Building
Christian
Communities
for Justice

THE FAITH EXPERIENCE BOOK

Building Christian Communities for Justice

Paul Roy, S. J.

 PAULIST PRESS   New York/Ramsey

Acknowledgements
My thanks are due to the following publishers for permission to quote from the works cited: Selections from *Mater et Magistra* (MM), translated by William J. Gibbons, S.J., *et al.* Copyright © 1961 by Paulist Press. Used with permission. Selections from *The Documents of Vatican II (Message to Humanity*-MH; *Gaudium et Spes*-GS; *Lumen Gentium*-LG), edited by Walter Abbott, S.J. Copyright © 1966 by America Press, Inc. Used with permission. Selections from *Pacem in Terris* (PT). Copyright © 1963 by America Press, Inc. Used with permission. Selections from the Medellín Conference, taken from "The Church in the Present-Day Transformation of Latin America in the Light of the Council," Vol. 2, *Conclusions.* Copyright © 1970 by the Latin American Bureau of the USCC and the General Secretariat of the Latin American Episcopal Conference. Used with permission. Selections from *Octogesima Adveniens* (OA) and *Justice in the World* (JW). Copyright © by the Vatican Polyglot Press. Used with permission. All scriptural quotations (unless otherwise noted) are from *The Holy Bible, Revised Standard Version.* Copyright © 1972 by Thomas Nelson, Inc. Used with permission. Excerpts from *On the Development of Peoples* (1967), *To Do the Work of Justice—A Plan of Action for the Catholic Community in the United States* (1978), and *Redemptor Hominis* (RH) (1979) are reprinted with permission of the United States Catholic Conference.

Library of Congress
Catalog Card Number: 81-80050

ISBN: 0-8091-2380-0

Published by Paulist Press
545 Island Road, Ramsey, N.J. 07446

Printed and bound in the
United States of America

Table of Contents

   This is a time of faith sharing based on our experience of the Beatitudes. The first part of this chapter
   will look at Christ in terms of the way he describes
   himself when he instructs his disciples, and at what
   blessedness and blessing have to do with the way we
   live our lives. The second part of the chapter is the
   explanation of the faith experience format.

   The question of the connection between faith and
   justice is what is looked at in this faith sharing format. The chapter begins by looking at Christ as the
   faithful liberator, and the Church's social teaching,
   and at what might be an adult Christian stance in
   today's world.

The way we choose to live has a great deal to do with the way we will be able to witness to Christ and to do justice. FE VI involves people in faith sharing about lifestyle. The first part of Chapter 6 deals with: (a) Christianity as a radical approach to living, (b) need vs. choice vs. Gospel, and (c) "style." Also included in this chapter will be a suggestion for a "Lifestyle Journal" to help people continue reflection on the way they live.

This chapter begins with a reflection on prayer as "honesty, presence, and response," and then provides a format for faith sharing on a regular basis. It is based on the Examen from the *Spiritual Exercises of St. Ignatius*, and can be used as a prayer at a weekly gathering if the members of a group wish to engage in regular faith sharing.

The Faith Experience is a community building tool developed originally by a CLC member for this movement. The communities try to live a spirituality that flows from the *Spiritual Exercises* and from the kind of shared experience of God that leads to dynamic service in the world. This chapter is intended to let people know a bit more about this movement.

DEDICATION

In Thanksgiving
to my Mother and Father
whose faith,
shared with me,
taught me to believe
in a loving God,
in those who people my world,
in myself.

Foreword

Of the many dilemmas facing today's Church, I believe that the greatest is the place, or, more pointedly put, the *mission* of the Church in today's world. Just a brief contemplation of that world reveals a distressing scene of suffering, oppression, poverty and enslavement that tempts us to wonder if the Church, founded by the great liberator Jesus Christ, has been paying any attention at all to the human condition.

But that Church, as witnessed through many courageous men and women throughout time and as recorded by the always prophetic social teachings of the Church, has, indeed, been constantly struggling to bring alive the Spirit of the Gospel as human history has been unfolding.

We could say that today's Church, by participating in this struggle to live out Christ's mission of liberation, is beginning to face a particular conflict that has been coming about for several hundred years. It is a conflict which confuses and divides the community of believers in a way that threatens effective living out of the Gospel.

Our experience in the Church is that people approach their God in two primary modes. There are many who develop an intimate relationship with God and identify their spirituality through prayer and reflection. The result is often an intense growth in faith, even an experience of conversion that gives their lives new meanings, new directions, new ways of being. They have, through this prayer ministry, called others to this new consciousness.

And there are others in our Church whose primary focus and approach to God has been through their view of the world. They have allowed themselves to feel deeply the suffering of their fellow human beings, to become rightfully angry at those structures which oppress and destroy, to identify with the people of Jesus, the poor. Thus their lives have filled up with responses to the things they have seen. They work to alleviate suffering, they challenge unjust structures and organize others to do the same, and they even choose to live with the poor, so as to become one with Jesus and his preferred people.

Despite the tremendous growth, the arousal of consciousness, the unbelievable good that has come from Christians focused in either of these groups, conflict set in and has been articulated. Those whose spiritualities have deepened through reflection and shared conversion have pointed out that activists are often shallow and unprayerful, as busy as they become when they "get involved." The activists have complained that those centered in prayer and spirituality aren't really doing anything while the world is crying out for relief and reform.

To whatever extent the accusations are valid, the argument and underlying distrust of fellow Christians are sapping energy from the mission of the Church. Of course, both "sides" believe that the Church should make a difference for all of humanity. And there is agreement that the integrity and power of Christian response is in the integration of spirituality and work for justice. It is that integration, that "middle ground" where reflection and response bring life to the Gospel, that is addressed in this book.

"Faith sharing is the proclamation of the presence of God in the midst of his people." Faith sharing is daring to view the world as the people of God.

Fr. Paul Roy, S.J. has endeavored to give us a way to bring faith and justice together in a place where they can be understood, nurtured and lived out. It is within the community of believers, in small communities of Christians who share their faith, that the place exists for the people of God to view their world.

Salvation history continues to be written because of the fact that God continues to be present now in the midst of his people. His presence is brought to light by the community as they reflect *together* upon God's relationship with each of them. That sharing of faith reveals their identity as *a people*, and where individual spiritualities are brought together in faith, the communal spirituality of a people begins to emerge. Collectively, they understand so much more clearly the mission of Jesus that calls them, and in hearing the Spirit, the community becomes animated and seeks ways to actively respond to that mission in their world. That mission, the Gospel tells us, is justice.

The Christian Life Communities movement, both internationally and in this country, has used the Faith Experiences to give our communities time and space to develop a shared faith life. Perhaps the most exciting part of communal faith life is the constant possibility of even further transformation and creativity emerging from the heart of the community. The nature of the Faith Experience affords this possibility. We have found that the faith sharing is made richer by a consideration of the theological and historical background which is the basis for each Faith Experience. In addition, the original inspiration for this kind of faith sharing, which was given to us by Jose-Antonio Esquivel, S.J., is one that draws us to acceptance of the faith sharing of others. Thus, the depth of sharing and the way we listen to each other creates an atmosphere of openness and mutual support that continually challenges the community to new insights into the implications of our faith, transforms us into new levels of consciousness, and dares us to seek the ways we are called to the activities of liberation and justice in our world. And not to be forgotten is that our experience of each other, more times than not, is a delightful one. We encounter each other lovingly and with a great deal of gratitude for each other's lives.

When reading this book, we might first just simply enjoy Paul's personal sharing of the dimensions of who we have been and who we are becoming as Christians. The dynamic of the individual Faith Experiences is community-building, and it is there in the faith community that the experience of the presence of the Father becomes animated by the Spirit of love. And it is in the community that we discover together the ways that we must participate in Jesus' mission of peace, liberation, and justice.

Molly G. Fumia
Los Gatos, California

Preface

*How tremendous are the faithful companions the
Lord has given me!
My greatest delight is to be with them.*

Psalm 16:3

Many things have gone into the writing of this book, and I have many people to thank. To name them all would provide the kind of litany that, in itself, would be encouragement to those who ask whether or not the Church is truly alive.

There are names that need to be listed. I want you to know these people and their inspiration to me over the years.

I am grateful to my family. My mother was the first person not directly connected with the publication of the book to read it. I'm not sure she realizes how much of her is in this work. My father would have read it, too, but I was able to get the manuscript to him only ten days before his death. I trust he now knows his part in the book. My sister, Suzanne, and my brothers and sisters-in-law, Roland and Gabrielle, George and Giselle, Bob and Beulah—and my eleven nephews and nieces—have much to do with my faith. They believe in my faith, and challenge it, and help me continually to articulate it.

I am grateful to my brothers in the Society of Jesus, whose spirituality I share and who care for me and give me life and help me to hear and respond to the Lord in my life.

I am grateful to my CLC sisters and brothers. It was through them that I first made a Faith Experience Weekend, and it has been through them that I have come to know and love God's people in a special way. Three communities in particular have helped directly with this book through their ideas, their encouragement and their support: the CLC National Center Community and the Trinity CLC (both of St. Louis) and the Pacem in Terris CLC (of Northern California). I am proud to count myself a member of those communities.

I also express special thanks to Sr. Virginia Rose and her community (Sisters of the Holy Names) at Villa Maria Del Mar in Santa Cruz, California. They provided more-than-generous hospitality to me while I was writing the book.

Finally, I feel I should share the authorship of this book with two people who are very special to me. One is José-Antonio Esquivel, S.J., who developed the original Faith Experience as well as Faith Experiences II and III. I have written more about him in the Introduction.

The other is Molly Fumia, a CLC leader and mother of four, who spent many hours hearing me out, discussing—and arguing about—every chapter and each new format with me, encouraging me during the slow moments of writing, and going over every page of the manuscript, making suggestions about content and grammar.

My gratitude to these two for their inspiration, support and love is only poorly and inadequately expressed in these few words.

Introduction

This is what we proclaim to you:
what was from the beginning,
what we have heard,
what we have seen with our eyes,
what we have looked upon
and our hands have touched—
we speak of the word of life. . . .
What we have seen and heard
we proclaim in turn to you
so that you may share life with us.
This fellowship of ours is with the Father
and with his Son, Jesus Christ.

1 Jn. 1:1–3 (NAB)

Our God is a God who makes himself known to us, who manifests himself, in the very events of our history. The people of the Old Testament knew that; their experience of salvation, of encounter with the God of life, was one which called them to faith and to a new vision of world and history and possibilities. They gradually came to hear—and to really hear—because they were given new ears; they gradually came to see—and to really see—because they were given new eyes.

In the fullness of time—our time—it was an event of history which constituted the full manifestation of God to his people. The word which God spoke to tell us of himself was spoken to mankind in Jesus, the most unambiguous revelation ever to those God had chosen to be his own. Jesus is the Word who speaks "Father"—who proclaims a saving and lasting Presence.

Faith sharing is doing verbally what the evangelists did in writing the Gospels, and what the prophets of the Old Testament did through their lives and words. It is the proclamation of the presence of God in the midst of his people. It is a sharing of the good news. It is a writing of salvation history as it continues to be lived in our day.

1

This is simple in theory. In practice, faith sharing is often made difficult because of attitudes and beliefs that have developed among today's people of God. For example:

1. It is difficult to identify God's activity in the world.
2. It is difficult to speak as though I were the special object of God's concern. And besides, my faith is a private matter.
3. When I think about it, my God is mostly a crisis God, and this means that when I try to share my relationship with God, I am likely to focus on what is most negative in my life. It's too depressing a prospect.
4. The pressure to share that is often associated with group sessions really takes the possibility of enjoyment out of faith sharing.

Perhaps, then, real faith sharing requires of us the following basic, simple beliefs:

1. Belief that my God makes himself known in history—my history—and that I must reflect on that history if I am to grow in discernment, i.e., if I am to find God in my life and know his will for me.
2. Belief that I can find non-crisis situations in which the presence of God has been real to me.
3. Belief that the call to share the good news is a call to the humble acceptance of the fact that I am, indeed, the special object of God's concern—and a humble acceptance of the mission I have to share that with those around me.
4. Belief that only if I can freely choose to respond to that call—and only if I lovingly grant that freedom to everyone else—can there be true faith sharing.

The pages which follow are intended to be a help to developing those kinds of belief.

That a person encounters God and enters more deeply into salvation history is an event that should be recorded. It is certainly worthy of being shared. That someone comes to believe in—to see with new eyes—a new world, and a history that has direction, and a self that can be a "mover" in that history—all of this is surely a cause for rejoicing and for giving praise: Blessed be the God of Israel, for he has indeed visited his people and set them free (Lk. 1:68).

Our God is a good God. Who can deny that or keep it a secret? This is the good news. And the kingdom of God is not "yonder," or two thousand years ago, or at the end of time—"for behold, the kingdom of God is in your midst" (Lk. 17:20).

The Faith Experience, as it shall be explained in this book, is a format for such faith sharing. There is a dynamic which builds during the sessions of the Faith Experience, allowing the participants to get to know one another at a level which is "different" from the normal, everyday exchange that is a part of our lives. The sharing in Faith Experience I, for example, progresses from introduction, through a recounting of one's salvation history, to an acknowledgement of the Christlikeness of those in the group. The time invested in Faith Experience I includes personal prayer and reflection, group prayer, participation in a celebration of reconciliation and in the Eucharist, "formal" sharing, and informal social get-togethers.

Six phases of the Faith Experience have been developed thus far. Faith Experience I (FE I) is a consideration of *salvation history* and our place in that history. In FE II, we look at the Church as we experience it today and as we dream about its future. We also reflect on how participation in the *paschal mystery* must form a part of the life of the Church if we are to be what Christ intended us to be.

FE III moves a step further by considering the *call* of Christ to each of us, and the *freedom* we need to truly respond. Contemplation of the call of Christ must lead us to a desire to be with him, to live as he did. One way of doing that is by living according to the values and promises of the Beatitudes. This is the theme of FE IV.

FE V follows on this by considering the relationship between what we believe and the way we act. Here we look at the connection between *faith and justice,* and we reflect on what there is in our own experience that can help us to live the Christian message of justice. Finally, FE VI involves us in a consideration of *lifestyle,* and how the way we live can affect who we are as Church, how free we are, how we pray, how we live the Beatitudes, how effective we can be in the promotion of justice.

The goal of the Faith Experience is not intended to be a "high" for which no follow-up is to be provided, nor is "gimmickery" the order of the day. It is neither a retreat nor a group prayer session. It is neither discussion group nor sensitivity session. It is neither therapy nor an extended period of introspection.

Its goal is not in any kind of pre-conceived effect, but, rather, in the sharing itself. The Faith Experience is simply a time set aside for people to come together to reflect on and to share God's presence in their lives—to proclaim the goodness of God—to seek to know him as he reveals himself in and through the lives of his people.

Through faith sharing, a community is created and deepened by the growth of individual members. The real result of the Faith Experience has been a growing awareness in each person of God's saving activity in his or her own life, an awareness strengthened by the witness of others.

While not part of its stated goal, however, participation in the Faith Experience can result in new realizations for those who share their faith in community. In an atmosphere of freedom and acceptance, faith sharing takes people out of the realm of ideas and into the realm of experience, and opens them to the realization that their experiences are just as valid and good as anyone else's; there is no need to explain or defend one's life experiences.

The Faith Experience can open a whole new way of looking at life. People see the Lord working in their lives in ways and at times they had never considered as such. Even the "negative times" can be seen as growth-producing when they are looked at as part of one's salvation history. Simply seeing one's life as a "salvation history" is, in itself, an enriching awareness.

Finally, these formats for faith sharing can help people to become better listeners. Because there is no verbal response, the individuals in the group need not spend their time trying to plan out what to say, which questions to ask, and how to assert themselves or their points of view. Instead, they can experience listening and presence as their response, their unique gift given in thanks for the verbal sharing of others.

THE TUNER

The one who will guide a group through the Faith Experience is called a *Tuner*. The primary task of the Tuner is to assist the sharing by setting the proper tone during each of the sessions. Because the Faith Experience is intended primarily to be a religious encounter—a serious reflection upon the experience of God in one's life—the context of the sharing should be prayer. The Tuner must, then, be careful to set a prayerful, reverential tone to the entire process and to each of the individual sharing sessions.

God works in different ways in the lives of different people. If the sharing takes the aspect of "oneupmanship," the end result of the Faith Experience will leave much to be desired. The Tuner must be aware of this possibility and obviate it. A careful explanation of the rationale behind each of the sharing sessions and a gentle reminder of the special quality of what is being shared could help eliminate that kind of temptation.

Because the Faith Experience involves a sharing of that which goes deepest in our lives—our experience of God—there should be a sacredness about what is shared. Part of the dynamic of the Faith Experience, therefore, is that there be no discussion of, or comment upon, what is being shared. The Tuner's responsibility is to encourage all the participants to simply listen to and accept each person's experience of God and his or her understanding of, and response to, that experience.

Sharing is legitimate and growth-producing only when it is freely entered upon. The Tuner should be careful to set the tone for the Faith Experience in such a way that the participants feel no constraint whatsoever to say or share anything at any given time. Sharing through presence and listening is sometimes more significant to people than mere verbalizing, especially when that verbalizing is the result of group pressure and not of a deep desire and willingness to share.

Finally, a good Tuner is one who is rarely heard from specifically as a Tuner. The person who performs that function within a group should set the tone, get the group within the context of prayer, and certainly pay close attention to what is going on in the group as the sharing takes place. The Tuner should then disappear so to speak, as a Tuner, and *simply be a full participant in the group.*

The pages which follow present the several phases of the Faith Experience. Included in each chapter will be the format for the particular phase being discussed, a suggested time schedule for a Faith Experience Weekend, pointers for the Tuner, and Scripture suggestions for use in setting the tone, or in liturgies, or for further prayer and reflection.

The seventh chapter is a reflection on prayer and includes a format for faith sharing that can be used regularly by small groups. This format is called *communal reflection* and combines faith sharing and shared prayer in a session that can be held in thirty to forty-five minutes.

The final chapter gives a brief history of the Christian Life Community movement, for which the Faith Experience was originally developed.

THE ORIGINATOR OF THE FAITH EXPERIENCE

The man responsible for the development of the Faith Experience as a faith sharing model (and who is, therefore, the inspiration for this book) is a Cuban Jesuit, José-Antonio Esquivel, S.J. In his work during the past twelve to fifteen years among religious and with CLC members all over the world, he has effectively proclaimed the good news of Jesus Christ by encouraging people to find that good news within themselves and to share it with others. He developed FE I in the late 1960's, while working in the Dominican Republic, and introduced it into the United States in 1971. Since then, he has developed the formats for FE II and FE III as described in this book. Fr. Esquivel and I worked together to develop and refine the communal reflection format explained in Chapter 7.

In 1977, the CLC movement in the U.S. gave Fr. Esquivel its bienniel "CLC Award." The following is what the presenter, Sr. Mary Ann Foy, R.S.C.J., said of him on that occasion:

This award is presented to an individual for outstanding service in the promotion, growth, and/or development of the CLC movement in the U.S.

The person selected for the CLC award in 1977 has been singled out for basic loyalty and persevering enthusiasm and devotion to the ideals of the CLC movement in our country, often when experiencing real personal difficulties and anything but popularity in so doing. Moreover, this individual has contributed immensely to our movement by personally developing leadership and calling forth many in the U.S. to participate in the Spiritual Exercises and to experience resulting personal commitment to the ideals of St. Ignatius and The General Principles of the CLC way of life. This person likewise has assumed the responsibility to call forth Jesuit superiors and peers in the Society of Jesus to the vision of CLC as an authentic Ignatian apostolic thrust and ministry.

(He) has served in the National and International leadership communities of CLC and has challenged both groups to an on-going awareness of their call to spiritual leadership and faith values above all other priorities, has called forth the movement in the U.S. to a more sensitive awareness of its vocation to social justice, has proposed formation models to our movement, and has encouraged models for CLC centers or houses, eventually to be realized at the National CLC Center in St. Louis (in 1976). Through participation in conferences for youth, for moderators, and for member groups in all parts of our country, this candidate has served as an inspiration, a model, a challenger and a "caller forth" of many individuals to personal holiness, to leadership and to enthusiastic participation in the movement.

This individual will long be remembered for his unique contribution of a faith sharing model—the Faith Experience Weekend—which has shaped the lives of so many of us and which has refocused our movement on the profound reality of Christ incarnate among us within the membership of our communities. Furthermore, we will never measure the effect of his influence on the Catholic Church in the U.S. through the inauguration of Ignatian Discernment/Faith Experience Teams which introduced many religious and priests to the CLC way of life and inspired them to develop CLC's as relevant forms of renewal and spiritual growth in schools, parishes, and other environments.

Fr. Esquivel was further described as a man of resilience, creativity, courage, hope and energy. I write about him here for two reasons. First, it is important to me that those who read this book and who take part in any of the Faith Experiences realize the debt of gratitude that is owed to this man for his creativity and his faith. Second, and more important, Fr. Esquivel is my good friend—one who has deeply touched my own life. It is important to me that you meet him in some way as you read about the Faith Experience.

1   *Faith Experience I*
SALVATION HISTORY

> *Praised be the God and Father of our Lord Jesus
> Christ, who has bestowed on us in Christ every spiri-
> tual blessing in the heavens! God chose us in him be-
> fore the world began, to be holy and blameless in his
> sight, to be full of love; he likewise predestined us
> through Christ Jesus to be his adopted sons—such
> was his will and pleasure—that all might praise the
> glorious favor he has bestowed on us in his be-
> loved.... In him you too were chosen; when you
> heard the glad tidings of salvation, the word of
> truth, and believed in it, you were sealed with the
> Holy Spirit who had been promised.*
>
> Eph. 1:3–6, 13

When we talk about salvation history, we generally understand that part of the life of our world that is talked about in the
Bible. The time of creation until the time of Jesus' life, death, and
resurrection and the formation of the first Christian communities
what I was taught constituted salvation history.

We Christians look to both the Old and the New Testaments as
the inspired word of God, and see in these the testimony of God's
loving care for his people. We see ourselves as descendants of Abraham and as heirs of the first-born Son of God, Jesus Christ. We see
ourselves as a people freed from slavery in the exodus event, and
called to a new freedom in the paschal event.

Our recorded salvation history speaks to us of events and of
people who have been the occasion of God's revelation of himself to
our world. I would suggest that creation, liberation and peoplehood
are three significant "events" from salvation history that have serious and exciting meaning for us in our day, and that the biblical
people of God as "interactors with God," as "interpreters of

events," and as "a community of believers" have something important to say to us as we move into the twenty-first century.

BIBLICAL "EVENTS"

The Bible begins with an attempt to explain the origins of the universe. All of creation is seen as the handiwork of God, and all is very good.[1] Human beings are seen as having life sources both in God and in each other.[2] That, too, is good.

There are other beginnings in the Old Testament. It seems that biblical writers were constantly looking for origins—roots—in an attempt to find meaning in life as they experienced it. The account of the flood and of the covenant with Noah,[3] the call of Abraham and the covenant with him,[4] the calling forth, through Moses, of the Israelites from Egypt and the covenant with them[5]—all are stories of new beginnings. And the stories continued—through kings and prophets. There were always new beginnings, always a new creation, always a new people. Yet there was ever the same covenant, ever the same origins, ever the same rootedness in the faithful God.[6]

The need to explain origins and beginnings was somehow intertwined with the need to explain the fluctuations experienced between strength and weakness, wholeness and brokenness, health and illness, holiness and sin among the people of God. For with the stories of glorious creation and covenant, of passover and peoplehood and kingdom, there are the stories of pride and jealousy, of murder and idolatry, of division and oppression.

The Israelites had come to know that their origins had something to do with being free. They were created in freedom, and somehow this freedom was something that eluded the grasp of humans. Freedom was only occasionally glimpsed by them, and then lost, through deceit or selfishness or other forms of inhumanity. Those occasional glimpses of freedom, consequently, came to be seen as hints of the destiny of all human beings.

And so, the stories of creation, in light of human experience,

---

1. Gen. 1:31.
2. Gen. 2:21–24.
3. Gen. 8:1–3, 15–17, 21–22; 9:8–17.
4. Gen. 17:1–8.
5. Ex. 34:10, 27–28.
6. 1 Sam. 16; 2 Sam. 7:8–16; Is. 42:18—43:13; Jer. 31:31–40; Ez. 36:24–32; Zeph. 3:14–20.

also became stories of liberation. A second great "event," then, became central to the experience of God's people. Along with concern for origins, which made creation central, there was concern for destiny, which made liberation central.

The prime event of liberation, of course, is God's deliverance of his people from the hands of Pharaoh. The Israelites, the chosen ones, the beloved, are enslaved and oppressed in Egypt, and God hears their cries and leads them to freedom.[7]

The events that surround the exodus experience became a divine statement of opposition to all that was evil—to all that was inhuman—in the world. While it might be possible to see our humanness as the source of all evil in ourselves and in our world, that event of liberation seems to be saying that, in fact, our humanity is the *locus* of our strength. (This is surely more clearly manifested in the incarnation, the transfiguration and the resurrection of Jesus.)

What is of great importance to us now is that our origins and our destiny met in that act of liberation. And our history came to be seen as a history of salvation. Our God, the faithful one, was a God who liberated his people—from slavery, from oppression, from injustice, from idolatry, from inhumanity, from suffering, from exile, from sin. And that liberation was given that God's people might be just that: God's people—human, just, loving, gentle, free, after the very likeness of their creator.

The road from origins to destiny often seemed a long and arduous one. It points to a third significant Old Testament "event": peoplehood. There is a process of growth described in the Old Testament wherein individuals, called by the Lord, deepen their humanity and become "conveners" of a people. Through great leaders, holy men and women (albeit sinners), the Lord slowly, painstakingly forms a people to be his.

This community was a cause of great glory to the Lord—as well as a stunning disappointment to him. It was an idolatrous people, a people that was never quite sure of the presence of its God, even though that God constantly revealed himself in one way or another. In a sense, it was a "panicky" people that sometimes didn't have the patience or the courage or the faith to throw itself into the hands of its God.[8]

At other times, it was a community that knew its God, and wor-

---

7. Ex. 3:7–12.
8. Ex. 32:1–6; Is. 6:9–13; Jer. 2:14–19; Ez. 13:1–7; Hos. 4:1–3.

shiped faithfully, and regretted its sins, and looked after its poor and widowed and orphaned, and depended totally on its creator and shepherd.[9]

One can, I believe, read the Old Testament with these three events in mind (creation, liberation, community) and come to a better understanding of salvation history. It is the history of a people, created and loved by God, who were able to look at their own successes and failures, their good times and bad, with the eyes of a deep faith—the faith of Abraham and Isaac and Jacob, the faith of Moses and Miriam and Aaron, the faith of Ruth and Judith and Esther, the faith of Isaiah and Jeremiah and Amos, the faith of simple men and women who waited for the fulfillment of God's promise, who waited for the fullness of liberation, who continued to see, in the small events of their lives, the gradual and sure meeting of origin and destiny.

Origin and destiny met, for us humans, in its most elegant and eloquent, in God's Word-become-human, Jesus Christ. This Son of God, born of woman, a person like us in all but sin, became the once-and-for-all liberator of mankind.

It is striking that the New Testament begins with origins, establishing the rootedness of Jesus, not only in God (Jn. 1) but also in the people of God (Mt. 1). It seems very important that Jesus was a descendant of Abraham and of the line of David. His genealogy was significant, because it had something to do with the richness of who he was.

St. Paul describes Jesus as the New Adam—the source of new birth for us. Jesus is the origin of a new humanity—one through which the divine can clearly manifest itself in the world.[10]

The message of Jesus was a message of new birth. It was a call to repent of our inhumanity, to seek our rootedness in the Creator of all, to turn away from the slaveries of this world and to find new liberation by becoming fully who we are.

Once again the source of our being is the end of our being. In Christ we are freed up for freedom.[11] In him we become a new creation, and realize again that we are children of God, and brothers and sisters one to another.

It is necessary for Christians, as it was necessary for the Israelites of the Old Testament, that they live the process of becoming

---

9. 1 Chr. 16:1–36; Jer. 31:1–9; Ez. 36:22–32; Neh. 9:6–38; 2 Kgs. 23:1–23.
10. 1 Cor. 15:20–28; Rom. 5:14ff.
11. Gal. 5:1.

a people. It is necessary that Christians find themselves bound to one another after the manner and mind of Jesus Christ if they are to realize these three events of significance in salvation history: creation—now re-creation in Christ; deliverance—now liberation once-and-for-all in Christ; and peoplehood—now Church, the body of Christ.

I emphasize these three "events" in the lives of Old Testament and New Testament people—creation, liberation and peoplehood—because I believe they represent three contemporary "events" in our lives. They are events which have become the focus of attention of many people in the last few years.

The American search for heritage, or "roots," is one of these events. We all have a history, an ancestry, and especially in recent times it has become extremely important to know, and to cherish, one's origins. In years past, when we reflected on ancestry, it seems that most of us were only able to go as far back as that time in history when we were the victims of prejudice, or bigotry, or hatred. I grew up in a Franco-American community and watched people abandon the French language that made them self-conscious. I'm sure that all over this "melting pot" country of ours, large groups of people were constantly apologizing for the extent to which they had failed to melt out of their uniqueness.

This is not true anymore. That uniqueness is part of the richness of life, and we are coming to accept and to rejoice in that richness. Because of this, life itself is open to all kinds of new meanings and new possibilities. The hope of a world that does not have to succumb to the self-destructiveness of prejudice is rekindled with the new fire of the acceptance of uniqueness.

And so, we search our genealogies, we trace our family trees, we get in touch with the richness of our heritage. There we find some of what we are about, some of who we are. And we are even moved to celebrate what we have found, to place it in history that it might live on and grow to fullness through us and through those in whose history we shall live.

A second phenomenon of recent times is the quest for freedom—for liberation from oppression and injustice. Surely people have always striven to be free. But the articulation of that quest, the unmistakable focus given by liberation theologians, by champions of human rights, by writers and preachers, by establishment and by dissidents, makes of this quest an "event" worthy of note.

The past two decades have uncovered many new meanings for freedom in this "land of the free." People have sought political freedom and religous freedom; they have grasped at moral and social freedom; they have worked, and fought, and even begged for economic freedom, artistic freedom, freedom from illness, freedom from ignorance, freedom from discrimination.

Very often the quest for freedom has been at the expense of that which had been sought. People with new-found freedom did not know how to live with that freedom, and either found themselves enslaved by someone or something new—or became oppressors of others. A prime example of that is the way our freedom to own things has become a source of enslavement to things and has created a consumer society which oppresses the poor by its greed and the rich by its overpowering allurement and tendency toward selfishness.

So, the quest continues. People *will* be free! Those who live under oppressive governments will continue to seek ways of freeing themselves. Those who suffer injustice will continue to find ways of reforming the structures that bring about these injustices. Those who find themselves shackled by chains of disease, or fear, or possessions, or poverty will continue trying to break those chains. The "event" of liberation will continue.

What we are learning—again—is that that "event" (liberation) which goes back to who we are at our roots (origin) will flourish most especially, perhaps exclusively, when we establish some solidarity among the people of this planet. We *must* identify with each other. We *must* share each other's lives. We *must* build a world community—or whole segments of who we are will die a tragic death.

Our awarenesses have expanded—our sensibilities have been fine-tuned—to a point where it is impossible for us not to believe that we are, every one of us on this earth, connected to each other. We live the same life. We are, indeed, brothers and sisters.

The "event" which must take place, then, in our day is the formation of a people. The phenomenon of community—whether of the encounter groups, or fellowship groups, or small religious communities, or communes, or groups of nations—is a present-day manifestation of the fact that peoplehood is a possibility, even a desire in the hearts of many.

What does all of this say? It might be that as history continues to be made, a people must continue to reflect on that history with the eyes and the heart of faith. As we have an Old Testament and a New Testament, perhaps we need more and more to write a Contemporary Testament—a modern-day reflection on the way God reveals himself to us as our origin and our destiny, through his fidelity to the covenant which makes of us a people.

To write (or articulate) such a Contemporary Testament, we must be a people of Testament. Biblical people, those of the Old and New Testaments, were "interactors with God," "interpreters of events," and a "community of believers."

BIBLICAL PEOPLE

It takes a certain degree of boldness to identify yourself as an interactor with God. In Old Testament times, one could not look upon the face of God and live. One was not even to utter the name of God. God was the mighty one, unapproachable, terrible, awesome, greatly to be feared. How could one possibly hope to interact with such a God?

Yet, throughout salvation history, we have startling examples of the kind of faith that allowed people a glimpse of a totally different kind of God.

Abram allowed God to change his name to Abraham and believed in God's promise to make him the father of a multitude of nations (Gen. 17:4). And he laughed at God's optimistic promise that Sarah would bear a son in her old age (Gen. 17:15). Later on, Abraham would bargain with God to save Sodom (Gen. 18:22ff) and obediently, faithfully, carry out God's command to sacrifice Isaac, the child of the promise (Gen. 22).

This man, Abraham, is called our father in the faith. We are descendants of Abraham. The richness of his faith is a part of our heritage. The boldness with which he interacted with God was testimony, not to his irreverence, nor to his self-sufficiency, nor to his disbelief, but to his deep, loving, faithful surrender to his God.

Naturally, others followed in his footsteps. Jacob, for example, wrestled with God through the night, and said to him, "I will not let you go unless you bless me" (Gen. 32:24–31). Moses, knowing that the Israelites would be slow to believe, pressed God for his name (Ex. 3:13–15) and went back to God for a second set of tablets, seeking at the same time the Lord's patience and forgiveness in behalf of this sinful people (Ex. 32:30–35; 34:1–9).

King David prayed and fasted that the Lord might spare the life of his first child, and when the child died, David

> . . . arose from the earth, and washed, and anointed himself, and changed his clothes; and he went into the house

of the Lord, and worshiped; he then went to his own house; and when he asked, they set food before him and he ate. Then his servants said to him, "What is this thing that you have done? You fasted and wept for the child while it was alive; but when the child died, you arose and ate food." He said, "While the child was still alive, I fasted and wept; for I said, 'Who knows whether the Lord will be gracious to me, that the child may live?' But now he is dead; why should I fast? Can I bring him back again? I shall go to him, but he will not return to me." (2 Sam. 12:20–23)

King Solomon loved the Lord, and prayed for wisdom, that he might govern his people well. And Solomon greatly pleased the Lord in that request. And the Lord told him so:

Because you have asked this, and have not asked for yourself long life or riches or the life of your enemies, but have asked for yourself understanding to discern what is right, behold, I now do according to your word. Behold, I give you a wise and discerning mind, so that none like you shall arise after you. I give you also what you have not asked, both riches and honor, so that no other king shall compare with you, all your days. . . . (1 Kgs. 3:11–13)

Not only patriarchs and kings, but prophets, too, were people of faith, who heard their God and were daring enough to interact with him. When God was heard to ask "Whom shall I send, and who will go for us?" Isaiah responded, "Here am I. Send me" (Is. 6:8–9). And when the Lord called Jeremiah, this one encouraged the Lord to send someone else:

Then I said, "Ah, Lord God! Behold, I do not know how to speak, for I am only a youth." (Jer. 1:6)

Some were ready, others were reluctant, but all were prophets. Ezekiel and Amos, Joel and Micah, Obadiah and Zephaniah—all interacted with the Lord. They spoke his word—his message—and proclaimed his presence among the people. And often they interceded for the people before God, always seeking mercy and liberation from the Creator and giver of life.

Salvation history, in some ways, is most clearly presented to us in the words of the prophets, who show us a God who is unbeliev-

ably faithful to the covenant, a God who continues to be God to his
people:

> Comfort, comfort my people, says your God. Speak tender-
> ly to Jerusalem, and cry to her that her warfare is ended,
> that her iniquity is pardoned, that she has received from
> the Lord's hand double for all her sins. . . . Behold, the Lord
> God comes with might, and his arm rules for him; behold,
> his reward is with him, and his recompense before him. He
> will feed his flock like a shepherd, he will gather the lambs
> in his arms, he will carry them in his bosom, and gently
> lead those that are with young. . . . The Lord is the ever-
> lasting God, the Creator of the ends of the earth. He does
> not faint or grow weary, his understanding is unsearchable.
> (Is. 40:1–2, 10–11, 28)

In New Testament times, there was a similar type of boldness
in the way people interacted with Jesus. Some of the Gospel stories
certainly bespeak a faith on the part of the "interactors" in the divine power of the carpenter from Nazareth who worked wonders
among the people, and who called God "Abba."

John the Baptist stands in the Jordan and argues with Jesus:
" 'I need to be baptized by you, and so you come to me?' But Jesus
answered him, 'Let it be so for now; for thus it is fitting for us to
fulfill all righteousness.' Then he consented" (Mt. 3:14–15).

Peter was one whose boldness only increased as his faith increased. Early on in his "career" with Jesus, Peter spoke to him in
this way:

> Then he made the disciples get into the boat and go before
> him to the other side, while he dismissed the crowds. And
> after he had dismissed the crowds, he went up on the
> mountain by himself to pray. When evening came, he was
> there alone, but the boat by this time was many furlongs
> distant from the land, beaten by the waves; for the wind
> was against them. And in the fourth watch of the night he
> came to them, walking on the sea. But when the disciples
> saw him walking on the sea, they were terrified, saying, "It
> is a ghost!" And they cried out for fear. But immediately
> he spoke out to them, saying, "Take heart, it is I; have no
> fear." And Peter answered him, "Lord, if it is you, bid me
> come to you on the water." He said, "Come." So Peter got

out of the boat and walked on the water and came to Jesus;
but when he saw the wind, he was afraid, and beginning
to sink he cried out, "Lord, save me." Jesus immediately
reached out his hand and caught him, saying to him, "O
man of little faith, why did you doubt?" And when they got
into the boat, the wind ceased. And those in the boat worshiped him, saying, "Truly you are the Son of God." (Mt.
14:22–33)

Much later, after the resurrection, the conversations were con-
sistent: "Lord, you know everything; you know that I love you" (Jn.
21:17). And the boldness of the interaction continued:

Peter turned and saw following them the disciple whom
Jesus loved. . . . When Peter saw him, he said to Jesus,
"Lord, what about this man?" Jesus said to him, "If it is
my will that he remain until I come, what is it to you? Follow me!" (Jn. 21:20–22)

Mary, the mother of Jesus, was able to show her concern for a
young couple and to "press" her son into providing for their happiness (Jn. 2).

Martha and Mary, the sisters of Lazarus, could cry with Jesus,
while expressing a profound belief in him as the Lord of Life: "Lord,
if you had been here, my brother would not have died. And even
now I know that whatever you ask from God, God will give you"
(Jn. 11:21–22).

A leper on the road could approach Jesus and say to him, in the
simplicity of one who knows what is true: "If you will, you can
make me clean." And Jesus could answer with paralleled simplicity: "I will; be clean" (Mk. 1:40–41).

A centurion, who had deep feelings for even his servants, was
given deep feelings for the presence of one whose authority was
greater than the paralyzing forces of evil that the world must con-
tend with. And so, he interacted with Jesus as one "under authority":

When he was not far from the house, the centurion sent
friends to him, saying to him, "Lord, do not trouble yourself, for I am unworthy to have you come under my roof;
therefore I did not presume to come to you. But say the
word, and let my servant be healed. . . ." (Lk. 7:1–10)

A Greek woman, so concerned for the welfare of her daughter and so convinced that the power of Jesus was great, engaged him in the kind of conversation that made it impossible for Jesus not to pay attention to her and to minister to her needs (Mk. 7:24–30).

The list could go on. The point is that when people approached their God with a real faith in him, in his power, in his love, then they could interact with him, be in relationship with him, let him be God in their lives, and discover more of themselves in the process. It seems, sometimes, that we are hesitant to interact with our God nowadays with that kind of boldness. One gets the feeling that people are afraid to "impose" on God, or to "burden him excessively" with their problems, or to "take up too much of his precious time," or to "bore him to death with my mundane life," etc., etc., etc.

The faith needed to be an "interactor with God," when lived out, was the kind of faith that led one to become an "interpreter of events." Of course, we always interpret events. We naturally try to find "rhyme and reason" for the things that take place in our lives. But to interpret events in the light of faith—that is quite another matter. To do that, one must even have faith in faith! This requires a boldness akin to that needed to interact with God.

The Israelites of the Old Testament had a strong sense that it was in their day-to-day existence that their God was to be found. To them, a flood was a flood, and it was more; a rainbow was a rainbow, and it was more (Gen. 9:14–15); a victory in battle was victory, and it was more (Jos. 10:42; 2 Sam. 22:47–49).

The search for freedom, the elevation of a king, a death, a birth—all these were real indeed, and they were more. For it was in these events of their history that God revealed himself. For this people, the descendants of Abraham, believing was seeing; and if one but believed, one could see marvelous things. One, in fact, could even catch a glimpse of God, and converse with him.

For New Testament people, the challenge was ever the same: believe that you might see. How often did Jesus touch people's lives and assure them that it was their faith that had healed them—of blindness, or leprosy, or paralysis, or demonic possession, or death itself! The call was always: believe the unbelievable—that it is still in human history, in human events, that God most fully and clearly reveals himself to his people.

And for us, in this day, the call is still the same: believe that you might see. We are faced with choices in our lives, we try to make sense out of the events of our world, we seek the face of God, we search for fullness of life. We are nourished by our faith—and we sense our blindness, our confusion, our emptiness, our searching. Our faith, often perceived by us as small and weak, is all too often stretched to its limits by our history, and we are, as it were, dared to believe. And when we are so bold as to believe, we too catch that glimpse of God, and become discerning interpreters of events and prophetic heralds of God's presence in the world.

God revealed himself to a *people*. That people, down through the years of its history, was not always a group that lived in great and quiet agreement. The fact that they were God's chosen people did not eliminate ambiguities, disagreements, differences of opinion, or any other difficulties that we, social beings, are likely to encounter as we go about our business of being social.

Yet, they stayed together as a people. They came to identify more and more with each other. They established a solidarity that was able to survive famine and war, slavery and exile, injustice and corruption. As long as they continued to interact with their God and to interpret the events of their lives in the light of their faith, then they continued to develop and grow as a community.

It was that faith that kept them together. The Old Testament people of God had a commonly shared experience of God that gave them the basis for their perseverance as a people. Not only did they have the faith of their fathers Abraham, Isaac, and Jacob, which gave them the ability to see God; not only did they reflect, in that faith, on the events of their world, which enabled them to understand signs and to discern God's dwelling place in their midst; they also had a willingness to proclaim to their brothers and sisters the wonderful works of God.

And in the days when Jesus Christ walked this earth, the need to be a people with a shared faith—with an "owned in common" experience of God—was no less present as a vital part of the existence of the people of God. The Israelites were again suffering oppression, this time at the hands of the Romans. Jews were, perhaps now more than ever, waiting for a Messiah who would re-establish this people in freedom and power.

Jesus, the Christ, the Anointed One, the Messiah, expanded the notion of peoplehood and tried to fight the false notions of his people about who this Messiah was to be and how he was to make himself known to the world.[12] The true liberator of mankind was to be one who proclaimed love and forgiveness, not hatred and ven-

---

12. Mt. 5:1–12; Mk. 9:33–37; Lk. 4:16–21; Jn. 12:20–32.

geance. The true liberator was to be one who proclaimed freedom to all because *all* were loved and honored and precious in the eyes of God. The peoplehood of God's people was to be rooted in the freedom of the children of God—for everyone, Jew and Gentile alike.

The Church as the people of God is a concept that has been made popular in modern times by the Fathers of Vatican II:

> At all times and among every people, God has given welcome to whosoever fears him and does what is right (cf. Acts 10:35). It has pleased God, however, to make men holy and save them not merely as individuals. without any mutual bonds, but by making them into a single people, a people which acknowledges him in truth and serves him in holiness. He therefore chose the race of Israel as a people unto himself. With it he set up a covenant. Step by step he taught this people by manifesting in its history both himself and the decree of his will, and making it holy unto himself. All these things, however, were done by way of preparation and as a figure of that new and perfect covenant which was to be ratified in Christ, and of that more luminous revelation which was to be given through God's very Word made flesh. (Lumen Gentium, n. 9)

While the concept has been popularized, still we are not a people. The reality is still missing among Christians. The force of an "owned-in-common" experience of God is still not felt in our world. The faith we have is, by and large, a private faith. The world does not hear of the marvelous, wonderful works of God because too large a number of God's people do not proclaim the good news of salvation.

We are descendants of Abraham. Our faith is the faith of Abraham and Isaac and Jacob, because their God is our God. Our faith is the faith of Peter, James, and John, because their God is our God, too. And there is some kind of logic to that faith.

The logic is that history is still being made—and that God must still be active in that history. We are still a people who are searching, who are looking for our origins, our roots, in the hope of finding there some basic, profound meaning in life, in our lives.

We are still a people seeking liberation. We want freedom. We feel deeply our lack of freedom, the various forms of slavery under which we struggle, and we catch occasional glimpses of what it means to be truly free.

We are still a people needing growth, and we are becoming more and more aware that growth is possible only when all grow. It is a global affair, or it simply does not take place. This means that we are still a people needing to become a people.

The Christians of the first Christian communities were described as being made bold by the Pentecost event:

> And when they had prayed, the place in which they were gathered together was shaken; and they were all filled with the Holy Spirit and spoke the word of God with boldness. (Acts 4:31)

We, in our day, are caught up in a progression of events which need to be looked at in the light of faith if we are to speak the word of God with the same kind of boldness. The news of the day is often that of war and death, of crime and corruption, of "simple" dishonesty and exploitation. In the newspapers, I read of the latest government money scandal (the largest in our country's history), and of the fighting in Nicaragua. There was a gang fight in a U.S. city which led to the massacre of five persons. There were strikes by school bus drivers, and by teachers, and by firemen (who stood by as a city block burned to the ground), and by policemen. A town in California was invaded by crickets. A woman was on trial for performing an abortion on herself. (She was later acquitted on grounds of insanity.) House investigators accused the Energy Department of concealing forecasts of a potentially dangerous gasoline shortage.

And even if we find it buried in the back pages, there is good news, too. There are events which are brilliant examples of people caring for each other, or trying to give life to others. There is goodness at work in the world.

There is a new Pentecost in our day! We are, perhaps more than in recent years, willing to be bold in our proclamation of the good news. There are some who are not embarrassed by the way God works in their lives. (Blessed are they!) And there are some who are truly prophetic in the way they proclaim the presence of the Lord in the midst of his people. (Blessed are they!) There are some who are willing to suffer and die in the cause of justice and liberation. (Blessed are they!) There are some who would proclaim, in the name of Christ, that we must live in peace, that we must meet one another with the meekness of the Lord Jesus, that we must be merciful toward all. (Blessed are they!) And there are some who would give over everything in order to be poor with Christ and to live in solidarity with God's special ones, his anawim. (Blessed are they!)

Very often, the events of our city, country or world do not even touch us. We must make a real effort to reflect on the implications and ramifications of those events on us and on those closest to us. But further, if we are to be true to the call to peoplehood which is ours as children of God, if we are to be a part of that process wherein origin and destiny meet, then that kind of reflection must become a vital part of the way we live.

In turn, it will be our participation in the life of a people that will deepen our faith and our ability to interact with God. And it will be our participation in the life of a people that will sharpen our discernment, our ability to be interpreters of the events of our world.

The Faith Experience is a process which seeks to foster that kind of participation in the life of the people of God. It is a "sharing of life" which itself takes daring and a great deal of faith. It is a step which we can take toward a new kind of faith—one that is rooted in all of creation and justified in all of humanity.

FAITH EXPERIENCE I

The first phase of the Faith Experience is an invitation for us to look at our lives of faith and to situate them within God's plan of salvation—to see our roots, our beginnings, our growth as touched by the loving, gentle hand of God—to experience our whole being as truly sealed with the sign of God's love and fidelity.

It is important that the Faith Experience not be looked at as a series of unrelated exercises, but as an on-going process, the dynamic of which builds gradually as the sharing itself takes place. There are five basic sessions in this process.

Session I

The first session of this Faith Experience serves as a basic introduction of the participants to one another, and sets the stage for the remainder of the weekend (or whatever time frame is used).[13]

---

13. Experience tells us that it is generally best to keep the size of the faith-sharing group to between six and twelve people. If there are more than this participating in the Faith Experience: (a) Session I would be more profitable if done in one large group; (b) it would be advisable to split up into two or more groups (with one Tuner

The Tuner gives a brief explanation of faith sharing (cf. Introduction), and specifically of the kind of faith sharing that the group will be engaged in during the Faith Experience.

The atmosphere should be a relaxed one. It is the role of the Tuner to put people at ease (often simply by his/her own calm and relaxed presentation), to inspire in the participants a sense of the Lord's presence as they gather to share his life within and among them, and to instill in them a sense of deep reverence for the experiences and insights of each person as the sharing begins. In this way the participants can truly enjoy the time they spend together as they grow in their awareness of the Lord's active presence in their midst and open themselves more and more to the possibility that the Lord speaks through each of them to their brothers and sisters.

The guidelines for the time of sharing are simple, and they are most important: (1) Let there be *no pressure* on anyone to say anything at any given time. Pressure creates unnecessary tension and can be a hindrance to the growth in one's ability to share verbally with a community. It is sometimes a good idea for the Tuner to suggest an explicit agreement on the part of all in the group that "we do, indeed, respect each other's freedom to speak or not, and we will not bring pressure to bear on anyone during our time together." Sharing by simply listening has its own, very great importance in this process. (2) Let there be *no discussion* of that which is shared by members of the community. When questions, or responses, are allowed it often happens that participants are stifled in their sharing, and they fit the sharing to the questions that might be asked. There will be an opportunity at the end of the process for some kind of response to the individuals in the group. The important thing is that each participant simply *listen to* and *accept* what is being shared.

Once these two guidelines have been explained, the Tuner sets the tone for the first exercise by reading a brief passage from Scripture, explaining the exercise, and calling the group to a few minutes of silent reflection to pull their thoughts together. The

---

for each group) for Sessions II, III, and V; (c) if you divide into smaller groups, do not split up couples, i.e., a husband should be in the same group as his wife; (d) bring the small groups together for explanations of the Sessions; and (e) liturgies would, of course, be in one large group.

following are examples of Scripture passages which relate well to the theme of this session:

Ephesians 1:3–13	Matthew 13:24–30
Exodus 3:1–16	Mark 9:2–8
Matthew 1:1–16	Luke 3:23–38
2 Chronicles 6:12–20	2 Chronicles 7:11, 15–16

The participants are asked now to share two things: (1) their expectations for this time of sharing, and (2) their genealogy. For the expectations, it seems best simply to ask all present "in turn" to express to the others what it is that brought them to this Faith Experience, what they hope will happen during the time of sharing, what their expectations are of the Faith Experience. Sharing in turn assures the Tuner that expectations will be heard from everyone. This is not so that the structure of the weekend might be altered in any way to meet all of the expectations (that would probably be impossible to do anyway), but rather to focus, for the Tuner and for the participants, what the needs are for them and for the group. For example, several people might say that one of their expectations is that they will have time to be alone. Then the period set aside for personal prayer after Session III becomes more of a significant part of the dynamic of the Faith Experience, and people take more of an advantage of that time.

After the expectations have been voiced, the participants are asked to share their genealogies. From this point on, the sharing is not done "in turn." Anyone may begin, and all are invited to speak when they are ready, or when the Spirit so moves them.

Genealogy simply means placing yourself in your own salvation history. Who are your parents, grandparents, family? What is your ethnic heritage? Where and when were you born? What schools did you attend? What did you study? What is your present line of study or work? And so on. This should be a skeletal presentation and should not be concerned with or include a sharing of experiences of one's faith life. The genealogy is an introduction—a way of beginning to see our lives in the light of faith.

After this initial sharing, the group might spend a few minutes in shared prayer. The Tuner should be aware of the ease, or lack thereof, with which the group enters into shared prayer. If necessary, the Tuner could give a few pointers about involvement in this communal form of praying.

This brings to an end the first session of the Faith Experience. It is good at this point for the participants to get together for a while in a more informal setting, and (especially if the group is going through this process during a weekend) to get a good night's sleep in preparation for the next day's activities.

Sessions II and III

It is during Sessions II and III that the sharing of faith experiences takes place. In the genealogy, the participants looked back to their roots—to their insertion into salvation history. Now they are asked to consider and to share elements in their own lives which constitute a "personal salvation history." How has God entered into their lives, acted in them, been present to them, worked through them? What events in their lives might be called "God moments"? What people, places, things in their lives have spoken to them of God? What is the good news of their lives? How is the Contemporary Testament being written in them?

The tendency, when such questions are asked, is to begin looking for what might be called "peak experiences" of one's life. (Have I ever been knocked off my horse, like St. Paul? Have I had a conversion experience analogous to St. Peter's? Has my Lord ever spoken to me through a burning bush?)

This is not the point of the Faith Experience. It is perhaps not even the way God generally reveals himself to his people. Rather, we look back at, reflect upon, remember the day-to-day experiences, the glimpses of God's presence in our lives. We seek in the small, the ordinary, the terribly human, a spark of hope which brings meaning to life, which allows the divine to manifest itself in and through the human.

Session II, then, begins in one large group (see note 13). The Tuner sets the tone for this session and the next by reading a passage from Scripture and giving a brief explanation of the faith sharing that the group will be involved in during this day.

Some Scripture passages that might be used for this are:

Psalm 139	Psalm 8
Jeremiah 1:4–10	Isaiah 6:1–13
Ephesians 2:1–10	Ephesians 3:14–21
Matthew 6:25–34	Matthew 16:24–26
Acts 2:17–18	

Participants should be asked, in Session II, to share faith experiences from as far back in their lives as they can remember up to, but not including, the last significant turning point in their lives. In Session III they will be asked to share that significant turning point and faith experiences from that time to the present.[14]

If there are more than twelve participants, smaller groups are then formed and the Tuner in each group rereads the Scripture and invites the people to spend fifteen minutes in quiet prayer and reflection before the sharing begins.[15] At the end of the fifteen minutes, the Tuner invites the members to begin their sharing of faith experiences. It is good at this time to remind everyone about the "ground rules" for sharing (no pressure; no discussion) and to encourage people to speak when they are ready, that is, without going around the group in any pre-determined order. It is also a good thing for the Tuner to say something about the value and importance of silence. Participants should not be afraid to sit together in silence for a while, to pull their thoughts together, to let what has been shared to sink in, to silently give thanks to God who does such marvelous things in the lives of his people.

Ordinarily, it will not be necessary to bring the large group together for an explanation of Session III. If these two sessions are taking place on the same day, it is likely that the small groups will be able simply to take up in the afternoon where they left off before lunch. If they have not finished Session II, then that is continued. At the beginning of Session III, the same procedure should be followed with regard to "tone setting," namely, a reading from Scripture (preferably different from the one used in Session II), an explanation of Session III, fifteen minutes of quiet prayer and reflection, and the sharing of faith experiences.

An important part of the Faith Experience is what we call a "period of synthesis." One hour should be scheduled after Session

14. If the group is made up of people who are settled in a particular state of life, a possible variation could be to ask the participants to share: (a) in Session II, faith experiences from as far back as they can remember up to, and including, the "dynamic of their vocation." This would include a sharing of faith experiences which had to do with their call to a state of life, whether that was a decision to marry, or to remain single, or to enter religious life or the priesthood; and (b) in Session III, faith experiences from that "point of decision" up to the present.

15. Depending upon the group's experience with shared prayer, it is sometimes good to invite them to spend the last five minutes of this period in that form of prayer if they so desire.

III to allow the participants to spend some time in personal prayer—reflecting on what they have shared and what others have shared with them. It is often necessary, and valuable, to have the time to "pull things together," to remember the remembering, to stand a while in awe of the tremendous goodness of God, to give thanks for this great goodness of the Lord of all, and to prayerfully prepare for Session IV.

Session IV

This fourth session of the Faith Experience is a liturgical "celebration of reconciliation." Up to this point, the participants have been looking back—to their roots and their heritage, to their earliest experiences of God, to the activity of God in their lives, to the various calls they have received from the Lord.

They have probably shared responses, moments of clear fidelity, times of great happiness and insight. And they have probably recounted times of confusion, darkness, and lack of response.

Now it is time to be in the present—and to be fully in the present. Now it is time to look at the possibility of integrating personal history into salvation history. To do this, the community celebrates reconciliation.

There are four aspects of reconciliation that we seek to emphasize during this celebration. As we look to our relationship with God, the consideration of call and failure to respond points to a need we may experience to be reconciled to this loving God, ever present to us, always loving, gently calling all to him.

As we engage in sharing our faith in community, we come to a greater awareness of the ramifications of our sinfulness as that sinfulness affects the life of the Christian community. Perhaps we experience, then, a need to be reconciled to those with whom we share our lives.

In addition to this, there is a sense of sinfulness that the community, as community, must come to terms with. We seek to express our common responsibility for the brokenness of this world, and to come to a deeper awareness of the forgiveness and healing which the Lord calls us to bring to the world.

Finally, an aspect of reconciliation which is generally forgotten is our own need to forgive ourselves—to be reconciled to ourselves—when we get in touch with our weakness and our failures and our sins. If we are to be able to accept the Lord's healing, and the peace of the Lord which comes to us through Christian fellowship, we must be able to accept ourselves as sinful people, redeemed and called beyond our sinfulness by Jesus Christ.

The celebration of reconciliation should include those four aspects. Generally, there is a consideration of the mercy of God as it is expressed in Scripture—a liturgy of the word if a Eucharist is to follow. Some suggestions for Scripture in this celebration are:

Isaiah 43:1–23	John 20:19–23
Psalm 51	Mark 2:1–12
Romans 8:18–39	John 12:20–32
1 John 4:7–21	Luke 7:36–50

A homily can be given to bring out the different aspects of reconciliation.

Following the homily, it is good to have a period of silent reflection, leading into a communal expression of sinfulness and need for God's healing. This can be done through a litany, for example, or in the form of a "prayer of the faithful." An example of such a litany is appended at the end of this chapter.

Individual confession, for those who wish to avail themselves of it, would take place while the community remains together in silent or shared prayer. A rite of peace is a fitting expression of the community's willingness to be reconciled to one another.

Regardless of the form it takes, this kind of ritual expression of reconciliation through litany, confession, rite of peace, or the like is an important part of this celebration. Our experience tells us that this is the most appreciated of the prayer times during the Faith Experience, and often the most important to a great many people.

After a joyful Eucharist, the community generally wishes to continue its celebrating. There is a new Spirit animating the group. A new plateau has been reached: we are in the present, reconciled, somehow more awake to the presence of the Lord in our lives and in our world.

Session V

The last session of the Faith Experience has two questions at the basis of the sharing and is generally considered to be the most beautiful part of the entire process. The participants have been in the past and have focused on themselves during most of the process. The celebration of reconciliation has brought the people into the present and has shifted the focus somewhat. The experience of faith is perceived as one which seeks the living God not only in one's personal life, but in the lives of all persons and in the vibrancy of all events.

The movement is from person to community, and to community as it is liberated and held together in Christ. The important question, then, is "Who is this Christ?" The participants are asked to share who Christ is for them at this point in their lives. What is sought is not a theological treatise or definition, but a simple sharing of that which goes to the very depths of our being. What is my relationship to the Savior of the world? Who do I say the Son of Man is? Who is Christ for me, now?

As at the beginning of all previous sessions, the Tuner sets the tone for the sharing that is to take place. Ordinarily, the passage from Matthew's Gospel, chapter 16, verses 13–15, is used. There is a fifteen minute period of prayer and reflection, and then people are invited to share. One interesting variation at this point would be to invite the people to do their sharing in the form of prayer addressed to Christ, wherein all tell Christ, in the hearing of the community, who he is in their lives. (This suggestion is only for those groups who already feel comfortable with shared prayer. Whatever form this sharing takes, the Tuner should encourage a special kind of prayerful, reverential atmosphere.)

After all have had the opportunity to talk about Christ in their lives, the final question is asked. It is, in reality, a completion of the previous question. It is also the time during the Faith Experience when participants have the opportunity to respond to each other. The question is: How do I find Christ in my life through the people in my life?

This last exercise is called the "Christ Seal." It is one in which the Christlikeness of each member of the community is acknowledged by every other member. Another way of asking the question is: What is it about each person that speaks to me of Christ?

This exercise calls the participants to give concrete testimony of the way God has placed his seal on the masterpieces of his creation—much in the same way artists place signatures on works of art which make those works clearly recognizable as their own. Or it is as St. Paul wrote to the Corinthians:

Are we beginning to commend ourselves again? ... You yourselves are our letter of recommendation, written on your hearts, to be known and read by all men; and you show that you are a letter from Christ delivered by us, written not with ink but with the Spirit of the living God, not on tablets of stone but on tablets of human hearts. (1 Cor. 3:1–3)

Here, concrete testimony is given of the ways in which we put on Christ through baptism. Here, people testify to the way Christ is recognizable in the world through the qualities of those who try to live and to love as he did.

It is best that a pre-determined order of sharing be used for this exercise. Call the Tuner Participant "A," and the others in the community B, C, D, E, F, G, and H. "B" can be the first to receive the Christ seal. This means that C, D, E, F, G, H, and A would each, in turn, tell B how B has spoken to them of Christ—what the Christ seal is that they see in B. (It may happen that the participants have known each other for a long time, or they may have been strangers to one another when they began the Faith Experience. Regardless, if sharing has taken place in the first four sessions, it will be possible for people to do this exercise.)

After all have spoken to B, it is C's turn. D begins to speak to C, followed by E, F, G, etc. All speak to C, and then E begins the circle speaking to D. And so it goes, until finally all have had a chance to speak to A.

It is a natural thing to want to pray together, or to celebrate the Eucharist after the kind of sharing that has taken place in these two exercises of Session V. That prayer, or liturgical celebration, brings to an end the Faith Experience. Hopefully, all have had a chance to experience a growth in their own faith and to see a bit more clearly how our good God continues to fill us with his life.

The following is a synopsis of the Faith Experience I (Salvation History) as it fits into a weekend schedule.

SESSION I

Friday Evening—7:30–9:00

(a) The Tuner gives a short introduction to faith sharing and sets down some basic guidelines for the weekend.

(b) The Tuner then sets the tone for the first exercise.

(c) Initial Sharing: (1) Expectations; (2) Genealogy; (3) Shared Prayer. It is good to follow this first session with an informal get-together.

SESSION II

Saturday Morning—9:00–12:00

(a) The Tuner sets the tone for the morning exercise.
(b) Fifteen minutes of prayer.
(c) Sharing of early faith experiences—usually up to, but not including, a significant turning point, e.g., one's choice of a state of life.

SESSION III

Saturday Afternoon—2:00–5:00

(a) The Tuner sets the tone for the afternoon exercise.
(b) Fifteen minutes of prayer.
(c) Sharing of faith experiences from turning point to the present. It is recommended that one hour (from 5:00 to 6:00) be used as a period of synthesis. This is a time for the participants to engage in personal reflection and prayer in order to bring together the various things that have been shared by the group.

SESSION IV

Saturday Evening—7:30–9:00

(a) The Tuner sets the tone for the evening exercise. This should include an explanation of the place of this celebration within the whole process of the Faith Experience.
(b) Celebration of reconciliation.
(c) Eucharist. Here, again, it is good to follow this evening's celebration with a party.

SESSION V

Sunday Morning—9:00–12:00

(a) The Tuner sets the tone for the morning exercise.
(b) Sharing on "Who is Christ for me now?" This may be done in the context of a shared prayer, or following the usual fifteen-minute period of prayer.

(c) Sharing on "What I see of Christ in you." This exercise is called "The Christ Seal."

(d) Closing Eucharistic celebration.

A COMMUNAL EXPRESSION OF SINFULNESS

This type of prayer is an example of a litany that could be used during the celebration of reconciliation.

LEADER (L): The world is broken because we disorder our relationships with God, with other people, with things, with ourselves. Let us pray for healing and a rising from death to life—for ourselves and for the world. For the times we have not let God be God, but have made idols of money, status, material possessions, ideas, and ourselves, we pray for the healing of God's forgiveness.

RESPONSE (R): Lord, forgive us.

L: For the times we have not been true to ourselves, but have given way to discouragement, despair, and a spirit of hopelessness, we pray for the healing of God's forgiveness.

R: Lord, forgive us.

L: For the times we have not been true to the people around us, but have engaged in play-acting, in phoniness and deceit, we pray for the healing of God's forgiveness.

R: Lord, forgive us.

L: For the times when pride has kept us from being of service, prejudice has kept us from being accepting, selfishness has kept us from being giving, and hardness of heart has kept us from forgiving our neighbor, we pray for the healing of God's forgiveness.

R: Lord, forgive us.

L: For the times we have enslaved people by our attitudes, and oppressed people by our carelessness, or neglected people by our callousness, we pray for the healing of God's forgiveness.

R: Lord, forgive us.

L: For the times we have failed to be aware of the suffering around us—for the times our awareness has failed to make us care—for the times our caring has failed to make us healers—we pray for the healing of God's forgiveness.

R: Lord, forgive us.

L: For the times we have failed to contribute to the resurrection of this broken world—by not feeding the hungry, clothing the naked, caring for the aged, the sick, the lonely, the imprisoned, consoling those in sorrow, giving freedom to the oppressed, making peace, taking care of God's beautiful creation: air, water, and land—we pray for the healing of God's forgiveness.

R: Lord, forgive us.

2

Faith Experience II

THE CHURCH AND THE WORLD

*The hour has come for the Son of Man to be glori-
fied. Truly, truly, I say to you, unless a grain of
wheat falls into the earth and dies, it remains alone;
but if it dies, it bears much fruit. He who loves his
life loses it, and he who hates his life in this world
will keep it for eternal life. If anyone serves me, he
must follow me; and where I am, there shall my servant be also; if anyone serves me, the Father will
honor him. . . . And I, when I am lifted up from the
earth, will draw all men to myself.*

Jn. 12:23–26, 32

Our faith in God and our faith in the Lord Jesus Christ necessarily lead us to participation in a body of people who, through that
same faith, are brought together as *Church*. The testimony of the
apostles leaves no doubt that Jesus specifically intended his followers to form an ecclesial community. When Peter acknowledged Jesus as "the Christ, the Son of the living God," Jesus called him
Rock, and assured him: "On this rock I will build my Church. . . ."
(Mt. 16:13–20).

And so he has built his Church, this group of people described
by the Fathers of Vatican II (Lumen Gentium, nn. 6–9) as:

- a sheepfold whose one and necessary door is Christ (Jn. 10:1–
  10)
- a tract of land to be cultivated, the field of God (1 Cor. 3:9)
- the edifice of God . . . the new Jerusalem . . . our Mother . . .
  the spotless spouse of the spotless Lamb . . . (1 Cor. 3:9; Gal.
  4:26; Rev. 12:17; 19:7; 21:2, 9; 22:17)
- the people of God (1 Pet. 2:9–10)

As the Church began its growth after the death and resurrection of Jesus, three things were required for membership: faith in the Lordship of Jesus, belief in the Gospel (good news) proclaimed by Jesus, and baptism into the death and resurrection of Jesus. These three requirements established a person in a special relationship with Jesus and with all others who belonged to this community of believers.

All who accepted, in faith, the Lordship of Jesus accepted him as risen Savior and therefore as the cause of their personal salvation (Acts 2:36). Belief in the Gospel brought them one step further, because belief implied active participation in the message of Jesus. Believers, therefore, sought to put on the mind of Christ, to live as Jesus did (in fidelity to the Father), to deal mercifully with all, and to show a special concern for, even an identification with, the poor and the oppressed (Lk. 4:16–27). Baptism plunged them into the depths of the mystery of Christ. He who had died was now risen and called all to participate, through his Spirit, in this new life (Acts 2:37–38); all were invited to be vital, vibrant members of the body of Christ. The baptized became a member of a community whose goal was to be faithful to the Gospel and to live and grow under the Lordship of Jesus Christ (Acts 2:43–47).

Structure, mission, worship, hierarchy, witness, sacraments—all had a great deal to do with the growth and development of the early Church. These things are still important. We are still trying to find ways in which we, as Church, can more effectively respond to the call of Christ.

> Christ, the one Mediator, established and ceaselessly sustains here on earth his holy Church, the community of faith, hope, and charity, as a visible structure. Through it he communicates truth and grace to all. . . . Just as Christ carried out the work of redemption in poverty and under oppression, so the Church is called to follow the same path in communicating to men the fruits of salvation. Christ Jesus, "though he was by nature God . . . emptied himself, taking the nature of a slave" (Phil. 2:6), and, "being rich, he became poor" (2 Cor. 8:9) for our sakes. Thus, although the Church needs human resources to carry out its mission, it is not set up to seek earthly glory, but to proclaim humility and self-sacrifice, even by its own example. (Lumen Gentium, n. 8)

Let us briefly reflect on three aspects of Church that might help us to remain faithful to Christ, who is head of the Church. Let us look at Church as (a) the assembly that remembers Jesus, (b) the people who put on the mind of Christ, and (c) the community that lives the paschal mystery.

THE ASSEMBLY THAT REMEMBERS JESUS

Memory is such a tremendous gift! It is re-creative. Of greatest importance to the early Christians was that they used that gift to remember and to re-create those unbelievable events that had filled their lives with wonder. Jesus had walked among them. He had done so many marvelous things. He had said so much about what it meant to be a follower of his—to be a member of his Church. He had shown them so often what the power of God really was, and had told them so much about this just and loving God.

More than that, he had promised he would be present, "where two or three are gathered in my name" (Mt. 18:20). And he asked them, specifically as Church, to remember him:

And when the hour came, he sat at table and the apostles with him. And he said to them, "I have earnestly desired to eat this passover with you before I suffer; for I tell you, I shall not eat it until it is fulfilled in the kingdom of God." And he took a cup, and when he had given thanks he said, "Take this, and divide it among yourselves; for I tell you that from now on I shall not drink of the fruit of the vine until the kingdom of God comes." And he took bread, and when he had given thanks he broke it and gave it to them, saying, "This is my body which is given for you. Do this in remembrance of me." And likewise the cup after supper, saying, "This cup which is poured out for you is the new covenant in my blood. . . ." (Lk. 22:14–20)

For us, the Gospels represent some of that remembering. The evangelists recorded events in the life of Jesus, or things that Jesus taught his people, so that that people—and all who would follow—might not forget, so that all would keep ever before them the memory of this man in whose Spirit they walked.

In addition to the Gospels (and the word-of-mouth tradition whereby things about Jesus were handed down), the early Christians had their liturgical celebrations—especially the Eucharist. It had long been an integral part of the worship of the Israelites to remember and recount the saving deeds of God, the deliverance of his people from Egypt (see Ex. 12:1–20; Dt. 11:18–25).

Now Christ represented the new Moses, and his death and resurrection was a new passover; a new liberation was effected among the people; a new covenant was established, through the body and blood of the Lord.

In the Eucharist was summed up the whole life of the Church which Christ established on this earth. For in the Eucharist there was: (1) a community (2) gathered in the name of Jesus, (3) breaking bread, (4) praising God, (5) remembering God's deliverance of his people in Jesus Christ, and (6) going forth to live the implications— the mission—of that dynamic remembering.

Ideally, that is still what the Eucharist is for Christians today. Ideally, when we participate in the Eucharist, we are most *Church*—a people rooted in Jesus Christ, remembering joyfully, gratefully, our liberation because "Christ has died, Christ is risen, Christ will come again," and going forth to live the implications of that good news—that great mystery of our faith.

Of course, there are other times of remembering. The Faith Experience explained in the previous chapter is an example of that kind of time. Our prayer, whether individual or communal, can be a time of remembering. Simply talking with a friend can be an occasion for remembering.

The important thing is that we remember and keep alive in us the memory of God's work in our lives, and that we share the good news with our brothers and sisters. For this is a deeply significant part of who we are as Church: an assembly that remembers Jesus.

THE PEOPLE WHO PUT ON THE MIND OF CHRIST

Jesus Christ called his followers to a dynamic memory—an "alive remembering"—of who he was for them and for the world. He also called these simple, faithful people to "project him" in the world, to make sure his presence was still experienced even after his ascension. He called them to continue his work of healing, forgiving, feeding, teaching, and life-giving—to live in his Spirit that all might rejoice in the good news of a new passover and of a new liberation.

For the early Christians to do that, it was necessary that they put on the mind of Christ (Phil. 2:5–11). They had to let that Word-made-flesh become so much a part of them that they became an echo of that word—a rearticulation of it. They had to so identify with their Lord that they would be able to meet people as he did, and speak in his name, and do the great things that he did—and even more (Jn. 14:12).

What does it mean to "put on the mind of Christ"? It must mean, at least, to accept as one's own the values by which Jesus lived his life. We often hear that the Son of God chose to become human and to walk this earth in order to bring salvation. Do we also hear, in that statement, that the Son of God *valued* humanity as the "place par excellence" in which the divinity might manifest itself to the world? Do we also hear that the Son-of-God-now-human valued life itself—*all* human life—as precious, as something to be cherished and loved and cared for? Do we also hear that freedom, liberation, salvation, was something that Jesus valued—even to the point of dying to achieve it?

The mind of Christ, therefore, can be known in part by simply looking at who he was. It can also be known by looking at what he said and did.

We must ask ourselves, for example, whether Jesus fed the multitudes so that he could manifest his power, or because he was genuinely concerned that people not go hungry (Mt. 15:32).

We must ask ourselves whether his reading of the Isaian prophecy and his identification with that mission ("to preach the good news to the poor . . . to proclaim release to the captives and recovering of sight to the blind, to set at liberty those who are oppressed, to proclaim the acceptable year of the Lord"—Lk. 4:18–19) was simply an attempt to befuddle those who were in the synagogue, or whether those *really* were values that he held and whether that *really* was the work he was sent to do.

We must ask ourselves whether the Sermon on the Mount was an attempt to parallel the experience of Moses on Sinai (by giving "do's and don'ts to the people) and to tell the poor and the oppressed to "hang in there" because the next world held all kinds of blessings for them, or whether Jesus was really telling his people what he valued, and how he chose to live his life, and how he was inviting them to do the same, and how God would bless, here and now, those who live by those values for the sake of Jesus (Mt. 5–7).

The mind of Christ can be seen or understood, to some degree, by listening to the life of Christ: love one another, forgive seventy times seven times, be one in the Father and in me, love your enemies, sell all you have and give to the poor, you yourselves give them to eat, blessed are the meek, peace is my gift to you, let no one call you father or teacher or rabbi, don't judge lest you be judged, don't worry about what you are to eat or drink or wear, be compassionate as your heavenly Father is compassionate, seek first the kingdom of heaven, unless you become as one of these little children you shall not enter the kingdom of heaven . . .

The Church must be that body in whom God's word is alive and burning for expression (Jer. 20:7–9). It must be that body of people who have put on the mind of the Lord Jesus, faithful to the Father, living according to the values that give life and that bring glory to God in all ages and for all time.

THE COMMUNITY THAT LIVES
THE PASCHAL MYSTERY

The baptism of Christians was a baptism into the death and resurrection of Jesus. The remembering of the eucharistic community focused on remembering that same mystery of life overcoming death in Jesus. The most striking message of Jesus, that which most consistently came through in what he said and did, was that following him meant following all the way to Jerusalem and the cross. And following him to the cross gave promise of participating fully in the resurrection.

The paschal mystery—that mystery of the passion, death and resurrection of Jesus—had become the center of the life of Christians. It was *the* event which could lend meaning to the constant struggle they were involved in because of their determination to live in the Spirit of Jesus Christ.

St. Paul was certainly the most eloquent spokesperson of the early Christian community in encouraging the Church to "remember Jesus Christ, risen from the dead" (2 Tim. 2:8). The truth to be proclaimed was that anything could be endured because of the promise of Jesus Christ.

This was true of persecution for the sake of the Gospel:

Therefore I endure everything for the sake of the elect, that they also may obtain salvation in Christ Jesus with its eternal glory. The saying is sure: If we have died with him, we shall also live with him; if we endure, we shall also reign with him. (2 Tim. 2:10–12a)

It was also true for suffering of any kind:

> . . . we rejoice in our sufferings, knowing that suffering pro-
> duces endurance, and endurance produces character, and
> character produces hope, and hope does not disappoint us,
> because God's love has been poured into our hearts
> through the Holy Spirit which has been given to us. (Rom.
> 5:3–5)

It was true as well for the suffering that came from our sinfulness:

> For if we have been united with him in a death like his, we
> shall certainly be united with him in a resurrection like
> his. We know that our old self was crucified with him so
> that the sinful body might be destroyed, and we might no
> longer be enslaved to sin. For he who has died is freed from
> sin. But if we have died with Christ, we believe that we
> shall also live with him. (Rom. 6:5–8)

The call to the Church was a call to live in belief of the promise
of that great mystery. To be the body of Christ, the Church had
to live the life of Christ and the mystery of his passion, death and
resurrection—and it had to live that over and over again.

To the extent that Christians were able to live the paschal mystery in their lives, to that extent were they able to stand in contra-
diction to a great many "worldly" values. The "power" of the world
was rendered powerless in the face of human beings who were willing to sacrifice all—even their own lives—out of love. To the extent
that Christians lived the paschal mystery, to that extent were the
Beatitudes able to come to life in the Church. Living the paschal
mystery was in reality allowing oneself to be grasped by that freedom which alone could make it possible to "seek first the kingdom
of God."

TODAY'S CALL TO BE CHURCH

The call to be Church today is the same call from Christ that
was issued to early Christians. We must be an assembly that remembers Jesus, a people that puts on the mind of Christ, a community that lives the paschal mystery. And we must be all of that and
do all of that in today's world:

The joys and hopes, the griefs and anxieties of the men of this age, especially those who are poor or in any way afflicted, these too are the joys and hopes, the griefs and anxieties of the followers of Christ. Indeed, nothing genuinely human fails to raise an echo in their hearts. For theirs is a community composed of men. United in Christ, they are led by the Holy Spirit in their journey to the kingdom of their Father and they have welcomed the news of salvation which is meant for every man. That is why this community realizes that it is truly and intimately linked with mankind and its history. (Gaudium et Spes, n. 1)

We live in a world whose values often seem to be diametrically opposed to the values of Christ and the Church he founded. Many in our world today live with memories that are dulled by the arrogance that comes from achievement. They are blinded by the deceptive brilliance of what they can do. These are people who forget God altogether or who cannot see the hand of a loving Creator at work in this world.

Today's world encourages values that in many different ways do violence to the dignity of the human person and to the message and mind of Jesus. We grow up surrounded by expressions of a mentality that says that being "number one" is the all-important value—something to be achieved at any cost. The competitiveness of schools and businesses and professions, the insane nuclear arms race among nations, the "hoarding" approach to the world's goods, the unethical use of food as a "political pressure tool," the values of a consumer society, the violence of war, the violence of organized crime, the battle for "racial supremacy," discrimination on the basis of sex—all are manifestations of that mentality.

This is not a prophecy of doom. Those are, in fact, the basic values that "make the world go around." This is what we are caught up in when we get a job, or enter a school, or, for that matter, simply walk down the street. This is what determines national political policy, domestic and foreign; it is what determines our use of technology; it is even, at times, what "runs" our Church.

To speak to today's world, we must be willing to stand together as a counter-sign to the values that are death-dealing in the world. We must be a Church that calls the world to choose life, in the same way that the God of the Old Testament called his people to make that choice (Dt. 30:15–20).

That life, for us, must be Jesus Christ (Jn. 14:6). We must

choose Christ for ourselves. We must put on Christ, and live as Christ lived. That will make of us a different Church, indeed.

For then we will be a people with the *simplicity* of Christ. We will be a simple Church, with simple needs—a people who meet together in any way they can, in any place they can find, just for the simple joy of being together and of remembering together.

When we put on Christ, we will put on his *openness.* Then we will be a community that is aware of vast differences of opinion, yet unconditionally open to challenge and change.

When we choose as Christ chose, we will have to choose *insecurity* and *vulnerability.* Then we will be a Church whose only security rests in the knowledge that the call we hear may change without a second's notice; and we will be willing to risk everything on a hunch that to step forward and be heard will be, for that moment, a prophetic step.

We will be a Church that *yearns for justice,* that cries in the face of oppression, that becomes a healer of persons and of peoples. We will, in that quest for justice, choose *poverty* in order to more deeply and sensitively feel that yearning. And we will choose *freedom,* because we will be a people who understand the right to live and to breathe and to eat, and who give away those freedoms to those who don't have them.

Finally, we will be a *loving* Church. We will be, because of our choices, a warm, loving people who embrace each other and who, together, embrace the poor and the oppressed with a love that can only come from the life and love of God alive in us.

All of this means, too, that we will ultimately choose to be with Christ in his paschal mystery. We will be a Church of faith in the promise of resurrection. We will be willing to die with Christ so that the world may live. We will be able to laugh because we experience the joy of that great mystery: that in Christ, wholeness comes out of brokenness, healing comes out of illness, life comes out of death.

FAITH EXPERIENCE II

Faith Experience II is faith sharing on our experience of the Church and of the world in which we live. It is not presumed that participants have already done Faith Experience I, though we believe that the sharing in the second phase would be enhanced by the kind of reflection and sharing that takes place during the first.

There are seven sessions in Faith Experience II, and the role of the Tuner is basically the same as in all Faith Experiences. The "ground rules" for sharing are also the same, and it seems important that these be made explicit, even if the group has been together before. It helps to "set the tone" for the sharing.

Since Scripture will play an important part in this Faith Experience, the Tuner should be sure that all bring Bibles with them (or that there are enough Bibles on hand for everyone).

Session I

In the first session of this Faith Experience, the group of participants gathers in order to pray together. This is the beginning of being an assembly that remembers Jesus. Even if the sharing of later sessions will take place in smaller groups (cf. note 13 in Chapter 1), Session I should be done in one large group.

The prayer is focused on the immediate past of the participants and on how God has been active in their lives. The basic question is, "Where have I been, what has my life been like, in the recent past, and where am I now as I begin this Faith Experience?"

To deal with this question, all are asked to spend fifteen minutes in silent prayer and reflection during which time they would choose a passage from Scripture that best expresses how God has been/is a part of their life.

The sharing that would take place, then, would be a prayerful reading of the Scripture passage, a brief explanation of why it was chosen, and what it says to the speaker. (If the participants are not familiar enough with Scripture to locate a precise passage, they should nonetheless be encouraged to recount in their own words the basic idea of the Scripture passage they are thinking of. Often enough, someone in the group will be able to locate the text, thereby lending communal support to the experience.) The Tuner should encourage short periods of silence between speakers. This helps to maintain a prayerful atmosphere and allows what is shared to take root in the hearts of each.

After all have had a chance to share, the group might want to spend some time together in silent or shared prayer. This will often depend on how long the sharing has taken and on the physical stamina of the group. The Tuner should be aware of this and determine the amount of time accordingly. It can be as effective for the group to spend two minutes together in silence and then to praise God with a prayer or a song.

Session II

There are three parts to the second session. The first is an extended period of prayer and reflection on the experience of the early Church. The prayer should last from thirty to forty-five minutes, and it is the Tuner's responsibility to organize this prayer. Again, this would take place in one large group.

The purpose of this time is not to engage in shared prayer, but to get in touch with what Scripture tells us characterized the Spirit and the development of Church among the first Christians. It might be, then, that the Tuner would simply explain this purpose and read sections from Scripture, with intervals of silence between the sections. An alternative to this would be to develop a "Scripture service," with songs, readings, a homily, communal prayer (such as a litany), reflection, etc. It is up to the Tuner to decide what would be best for the group.

Some Scripture passages that would be helpful for this kind of reflection include:

Matthew 28:16–20	Acts 2:1–4
Acts 2:43–47	Acts 3:1–9
Acts 4:1–4	Acts 4:32–37
1 Corinthians 1:10–13	1 Corinthians 3:1–9
1 Corinthians 16:1–4	Acts 15

After the prayer, this Faith Sharing session is divided into two parts, each of which has a double question. Each helps us to focus on the Church as it is part of our lives.

The first of the double questions is: How do I see the Church today? and How do I see myself in the Church? Obviously, there are many different perceptions of Church among the people of God, and many different "ecclesiologies" are operative. The point here is not to produce *the* correct assessment or definition of today's Church, but to allow this community to share their experience of Church. (It is very important at this point that the sharing not break down into a discussion; the Tuner must make it clear that it is listening to, and accepting, the experience of others that is essential.)

The second double question is: How would I like to see the Church? and What would I like my place to be in that Church? In other words, what are my dreams for the Church and for myself in the Church?

The Tuner and the group may decide that they want to deal with the two questions together. There is no reason why that could not be done. The only caution is that when people do faith sharing on two separate questions (and double questions at that), one of the questions often gets lost. The Tuner should try to make sure that this does not happen—for example, by establishing a pattern of sharing that *clearly* deals with both questions.

It is recommended that the group be given a good amount of time (thirty minutes to an hour) to reflect on these questions before sharing. It is often helpful to encourage the participants to write down some of their thoughts and experiences and perceptions, and to use their notes during the sharing.

A short period of shared prayer brings this session to a close.

Session III

The third session is an exercise in imagination and creativity. In a sense, it is a small group synthesis of what has been shared, and so it should follow Session II without too great a lapse of time. If the group is making Faith Experience II during a weekend, this session would be fairly easy to do right after lunch on Saturday. If the group is doing these sessions in the evening, say once a week, this session might be difficult to go through. The Tuner should know the group and make a decision about how this session would be included in the whole process.

The instructions are quite simple: build a Church! The reflections and the sharing that have taken place have focused the participants on themselves as "Church people" and have encouraged them to dream about what Church might be. This session asks the participants to do that kind of dreaming in small groups rather than as individuals. What is it in all of this dreaming that we can bring together to give a communal picture of Church?

When given such instructions, people naturally think of making a collage that would represent Church for them. That is a possibility. But this is *not* an exercise whose goal is the production of a number of Church collages.

The goal is to have small groups (four persons at most in each group) spend a couple of hours coming to a common agreement about elements they would include in Church and finding some creative way of communicating that to all the other participants in the Faith Experience.

The session would therefore include a period of time in small groups, and a period of time when all are gathered in one large group to hear the results of each small group's work.

Session IV

The fourth session begins a consideration of the paschal mystery which will continue through Sessions V, VI, and VII. The movement of this consideration, and sharing, is from our experience of suffering and dying, to the Passion and Death of Jesus, to our experience of resurrection in Jesus.

In this session, the participants reflect about and share on the questions: What are the sufferings and dyings of the world? What are my sufferings and dyings? This is a kind of sharing which focuses the group on their perception and experience of how the world and they themselves participate in the Passion of Christ. This connection with Christ's suffering may not always be there. That is not important for the moment. It may be that, through this sharing and the sharing that will follow, the members of the group will be helped to make that connection.

Here again, it is advisable to give some time for personal reflection prior to the sharing, and to encourage people to write down some of their thoughts.

The Christian stance is one of hope and gratitude because Jesus Christ has overcome all evil and suffering and brokenness and death through his own Death and Resurrection. That is the promise of our God—and God is true to his word. We must remember.

This does not mean, however, that Christians should not remember, and experience in their hearts, the sadness of hurt that is still part of our world and of our lives. The remembering, in Session IV, is often painful or sad. The Tuner should be sure to maintain a prayerful, hopeful atmosphere (see Is. 53 or Mt. 8:16–17)—without attempting to "soften" the real feelings that are being expressed or experienced. There is no need to "protect" the community from this remembering of suffering and dying. Later sessions will show how this remembering sharpens our appreciation of the new passover and new liberation which are ours in the Resurrection of the Lord.

Session V

Church cannot be just a group of people who look sadly upon their world with a wish that there were more life in it. It has to be a community grounded in the firm belief that human experience is the "place" out of which comes fullness of life because of Jesus Christ.

Session V brings the faith-sharing community to a celebration of God's taking onto himself the sufferings and afflictions of the world. This is a time to re-enact, through ritual, that event which brought salvation to the whole world.

The "seder meal" is that part of the Jewish passover celebration in which all relive the exodus story, and the Holy Thursday evening liturgy is the reliving of the Christian pasch. Session V combines these two.

If possible, this session should include a seder, the Eucharist, and a regular meal. There are already a number of published Christian seder liturgies which can be used for this celebration. The Scripture used in the liturgy of the word on Holy Thursday provides a very good transition from the seder to the Eucharist.

What is important here is that an atmosphere be created which will help the participants to see themselves as a people who remember, humbly and with gratitude, that as God freed his people once from slavery in Egypt, so has this same God freed his people once-and-for-all from sin and death through Jesus Christ.

Session VI

The "Gethsemane experience" was for Jesus a time when he was able to integrate into his own life both the turmoil of what he was asked to do by his Father, and the peace which came from total abandonment to the Father's will. If we are to live as Jesus did, if we are to be a Church that lives the paschal mystery, then that integration must take place in us, too.

Session VI, which deals with the Gethsemane experience, is an extended contemplation of that event in Christ's life—a prayer during which the community seeks to "own" the paschal mystery in their lives.

There are five parts to this prayer. (a) The first is a reading of the Gospel account of the agony in the garden, which was recorded by three of the evangelists: Matthew (6:36–46), Mark (14:32–42), and Luke (22:39–46). (b) After the reading of one of these passages, the Tuner (or someone from the community) gives a brief homily stressing the importance of offering the sufferings and dyings of the world to the Father, of accepting to be with Christ in his death, and of keeping alive in all of this our hope of resurrection with Christ. (c) Next is a period (at least thirty minutes) of personal prayer. (d)

Then follows a sharing on the question: Where do I find (and experience) Christ's peace in myself and in the world? (e) The prayer and faith sharing are concluded with a sharing of Christ's peace (the kiss of peace) among the community.

Session VII

The paschal mystery is not the mystery of suffering and death. It is the mystery of healing and life overcoming that suffering and death. To complete our contemplation of this mystery, we must consider the Resurrection and its place in our lives. This we do in the final session of Faith Experience II. The session has two parts: an initial sharing, and a resurrection liturgy.

As the group gathers, the Tuner sets the tone for the faith sharing by reading one of the post-Resurrection accounts from Scripture. The group then spends fifteen minutes in prayer and reflection, considering the question: How does the Resurrection find expression in and through me? This will be the subject of the faith sharing—a personal witness of the way the risen Lord touches my life with Life and of the way I am able to respond by sharing that life with others.

In Faith Experience I, the "Christ seal" was one way of giving this same kind of testimony. Now, in our consideration of Church, it is important for individuals to acknowledge what gifts they themselves can bring to the life of the Church. (Later on, during the Eucharist, there will be a time for response from members of the community.)

The closing liturgy is one that celebrates resurrection. The liturgy of the word should center around John 21:1-19. In this passage, after the disciples recognize the risen Lord, Jesus cooks a meal for them, and then he asks for Peter's profession of love. This is a good time to make the connection between Gethsemane and mission: it is only when we agree to be with Christ, even in his suffering and dying, that we can clearly hear the call of Christ to live for him in this world:

> "Truly, truly, I say to you, when you were young, you girded yourself and walked where you would; but when you are old, you will stretch out your hands, and another will gird you and carry you where you do not wish to go." (This he said to show by what death he was to glorify God.) And after this he said to him, "Follow me." (John 21:18-19)

As part of this liturgy of the word, there should be a brief sharing during which participants acknowledge ways in which they are able to love the Lord—ways in which their love for God is translated into the activity of their daily lives.

Finally, Church is a people which goes forth from its worship to live the implications—the mission—of its dynamic remembering. This liturgy ends, therefore, with a special "blessing and missioning ceremony." All of the participants are asked to bless one another, to confirm the gifts each has spoken about (especially during Session VI), and to send each person forth to use that gift for the Church. This is most easily done in a manner similar to the kiss of peace, where each person goes to every other person in the community.

Hopefully, during this entire process of Faith Experience II, the community members have come to see more clearly the exciting possibilities of Church in today's world, deepened their understanding of the paschal mystery, sensitized themselves to the sufferings and dyings of the world, and come to believe more strongly that the risen Lord truly lives and that in him they contribute to the resurrection of the world.

The following is a synopsis of Faith Experience II (The Church and the World) as it fits into a weekend schedule.

SESSION I

Friday Evening—7:30–9:00

(a) The Tuner gives a short introduction to faith sharing and sets down some basic guidelines for the weekend.

(b) The Tuner then sets the tone for the first exercise.

(c) Prayer from Scripture: (1) Fifteen minutes of personal prayer and reflection; each chooses a passage from Scripture which expresses his or her present relationship with God. (2) Sharing: reading of the passage and brief explanation of why it was chosen. (3) Close with a communal prayer of praise or a song.

SESSION II

Saturday Morning—8:45–12:00

(a) Prayer on the experience of the early Church.

(b) Faith Sharing: How do I see the Church? How do I see myself in the Church?

(c) Faith Sharing: How would I like to see the Church? What would I like my place to be in that Church? These last two parts can be combined into one longer session. Time should be allowed for participants to reflect on the questions (and to write if they want to) before the sharing. This session would normally end with a short prayer.

SESSION III

Saturday Afternoon—1:30–3:00

(a) Church Building Exercise: work in groups of three or four to synthesize the sharing of the morning session. Instructions: build a Church, and find a creative way of communicating what you have built.

(b) Gather in one large group to hear the results of the small group work.

SESSION IV

Saturday Afternoon—3:30–5:00

(a) The Tuner sets the tone for the sharing that will take place.

(b) Faith Sharing: What are the sufferings and dyings of the world? What are my own sufferings and dyings? The group should have some time for personal reflection prior to the sharing.

SESSION V

Saturday Evening—5:30–7:30

(a) Seder/Eucharist/Dinner: these three celebrations should flow into one another.

SESSION VI

Saturday Evening—8:30–10:00

(a) The Tuner sets the tone for this session by explaining the prayer and by reading one of the Gethsemane accounts.
(b) The Tuner (or someone from the community) gives a brief homily.
(c) Personal Prayer (at least thirty minutes).
(d) Faith Sharing: Where do I find (and experience) Christ's peace in myself and in the world?
(e) A sharing of Christ's peace (kiss of peace).

SESSION VII

Sunday Morning—9:00–12:00

(a) The Tuner sets the tone for the first sharing by explaining the topic for sharing and by reading one of the post-Resurrection accounts from Scripture.
(b) Faith Sharing: How does the Resurrection find expression in and through me? As is usual in sharing sessions such as this one, there should be fifteen minutes of silent prayer and reflection before the sharing begins.
(c) A Resurrection Liturgy: based on John 21:1–19. During the homily, there should be a faith sharing session on the questions: How do I love the Lord? How is my love for the Lord translated into the activity of my daily life? The liturgy ends with a "blessing and missioning ceremony."

3   *Faith Experience III*
CALL

*I, therefore, a prisoner for the Lord, beg you to lead
a life worthy of the calling to which you have been
called, with all lowliness and meekness, with patience, forbearing one another in love, eager to maintain the unity of the Spirit in the bond of peace.
There is one body and one Spirit, just as you were
called to the one hope that belongs to your call, one
Lord, one faith, one baptism, one God and Father of
us all, who is above all and through all and in all.*
Eph. 4:1–6

God, who interacts with his people, is said to call them. He
called Abraham, for example, to be the father of a multitude of nations, and he called Paul to preach the Gospel among the Gentiles.
Every New Testament writer alludes to call as an important activity of God, and yet call is one of the most mysterious, ambiguous
aspects of our relationship with God. In what way does God call me?
Is call a function of our faith? Does it come from force of circumstance? Are we bound to respond? What assurance do we have that
it is really God who is calling?

Let us reflect on this by looking at: (1) calls in salvation history,
(2) the dilemma of call, and (3) response in freedom to the many
calls of God in our lives.

CALLS IN SALVATION HISTORY

From the very beginning of time, God has been "issuing calls."
He first of all called the universe into existence, and called man
and woman to be for each other and to complete the creation of this
world. This, at least, is one call that has remained constant for each
of us as human beings and as inheritors of this planet. The activity,

53

the very wonder, of creation constitutes a triple call: to be, to be for others, and to be creators and "completers" of God's handiwork.

In addition to "call through creation" we have clear examples of "call through covenant." The covenant with Abraham called the descendants of Abraham to peoplehood (Gen. 17), the covenant with Moses called that people to freedom (Ex. 20), the covenant announced through Jeremiah called that free people to "heartfelt, loving fidelity" (Jer. 31:31–34), and the new covenant established through the blood of the Lamb, Jesus Christ, called that people to be children of God: ". . . and if children, then heirs, heirs of God and fellow heirs with Christ, provided we suffer with him in order that we may also be glorified with him" (Rom. 8:17).

The New Testament speaks often of a third kind of call: "call through community in Christ." This call has been expressed in many different ways, but it generally directs itself toward basic attitudes and ways of living: love (2 Pet. 1:5–7; 1 Jn. 3:11); unity (Eph. 4:1–6), and ministry (Jas. 1:22–25). Jesus told his followers that his mission in life was to be lifted up and to draw all people to himself (Jn. 12:32), and his prayer was that all might be *one* in him (Jn. 17:20–26).

The faith of the people of God seems to have been a faith that enabled them to conceive of a God who would speak to them and ask (sometimes in quite specific terms) for their cooperation or collaboration with him. It is interesting to look at the "calls" received by a number of Old Testament and New Testament people, and to consider the ways in which God made himself—and his wishes—known:

> When Abram was ninety-nine years old the Lord appeared to Abram, and said to him, "I am God Almighty; walk before me, and be blameless!"(Gen. 17:1)

> And Moses said, "I will turn aside and see this great sight, why the bush is not burnt!" When the Lord saw that he turned aside to see, God said to him out of the bush, "Moses, Moses!" (Ex. 3:3–4)

> Samuel was lying down within the temple of the Lord, where the ark of God was. Then the Lord called, "Samuel, Samuel!" (1 Sam. 3:3–4)

4 And the Lord said (to Samuel), "Arise, anoint him, for this is he!" Then Samuel took the horn of oil, and anointed him in the midst of his brothers; and the Spirit of the Lord came mightily upon David from that day forward. (1 Sam. 16:12–13)

5 I (Isaiah) saw the Lord sitting upon a throne, high and lifted up; and his train filled the temple. . . . And I heard the voice of the Lord saying, "Whom shall I send, and who will go for us?" Then I said, "Here am I! Send me." (Is. 6:1, 8)

6 Now the word of the Lord came to me saying, "Before I formed you in the womb I knew you, and before you were born I consecrated you; I appointed you a prophet to the nations." (Jer. 1:4–5)

7 The angel Gabriel was sent from God to a city of Galilee named Nazareth, to a virgin betrothed to a man whose name was Joseph, of the house of David; and the virgin's name was Mary. . . . And the angel said to her, "Do not be afraid, Mary, for you have found favor with God." (Lk. 1:26–27, 30)

8 As he walked by the Sea of Galilee, he saw two brothers, Simon who is called Peter and Andrew his brother, casting a net into the sea; for they were fishermen. And he said to them, "Follow me, and I will make you fishers of men." (Mt. 4:18–19)

9 Suddenly a light from heaven flashed about him. And he fell to the ground and heard a voice saying to him, "Saul, Saul, why do you persecute me?" (Acts 9:3–4)

THE DILEMMA OF CALL

All of these people, in one way or another, had an experience of God which compelled them to risk everything in a response worthy of that awesome word spoken to them. How did they know it was God? How could they determine what it was they were being asked to do? And once they felt that they knew what God wanted, what possible assurance did they have that everything would "work out'"? Obviously, we can't answer those questions. But we might possibly conclude something as simple as: they just knew it was God, and they determined what he was saying by looking at the circumstances of their lives; they only had as much assurance that everything would work out as they had faith to know it was God who was calling them.

All of these people had at least three things in common. One was that they believed enough in God to allow him to call them by name. When someone calls your name—even in a crowd, even in the midst of noise, even when you are distracted—you *know* that you've been called. And when someone who loves you very much says your name, that person not only gets your attention, but touches your life. You know then that the deepest places within your heart have been reached. Something has suddenly come alive in you through the touching. And the place from which you know you are called and from which you respond is your heart. It is there also that God is wholly and profoundly within you. If that kind of calling can happen in our relationships with other human beings, why should it not happen in our relationship with God? What we need are the faith and the courage to search out that place where God is and where we gain a heartfelt knowledge of the ways and times God calls us by name (Jn. 20:11–18).

A second thing the saints of the Old and New Testaments had in common was that they allowed themselves to become totally immersed in life and in the world in which they lived. They were alive people—awake to what was going on around them. They were daring people—strikingly (because of their love of God) open to their own fallibility, willing to risk almost anything to be able to respond to what they knew in their hearts. For they knew that God was life itself and that total immersion in and total response to life was the same as fidelity to God. Indeed, it was becoming part of God! And it was in this very immersion that they could discover what it was that God was calling them to. The same must be true for us in our day. Isn't God still life itself? It is when we immerse ourselves most in life and in what is going on in our world that we feel most alive. It is also in that heartfelt living of life that we can most clearly make out what God is calling us to (Jn. 14:1–7).

And so, it is faith which is the beginning of our being called, and faith which must be the beginning of our interpretation of the call. The dilemma, however, is not simply in the hearing. Nor is it just a question of recognition or interpretation. Very often, the response itself is cause for a great deal of questioning and doubt. Here again, our faith must somehow develop a trusting heart in us.

The third thing our biblical people had in common was the faith which asserted that God's word would not be broken. To the extent that they gave a lively response to what they knew with their hearts, to that extent did they come to a clearer knowledge of God. And so, they could believe that God would be with them, that all would work out, that their fidelity to God would be matched by God's fidelity to them. So, too, with us; if we honestly do what we believe God calls us to, we must believe that he will be with us and that everything will work out (Rom. 8:28–31).

The lives of Abraham in the Old Testament and Jesus in the New Testament give us examples of how it is possible to hear clearly and to interpret accurately what the call is, and still find doubt, even sadness, in what must be the response.

Abraham was given a promise that his descendants would form a great people through his son Isaac. And Abraham believed that promise. He was given the assurance that he would live on after his death, that the special blessing of the Lord would continue down through the ages—all through Isaac, the child of his old age.

> After these things God tested Abraham, and said to him, "Abraham!" And he said, "Here am I." He said, "Take your son, your only son Isaac, whom you love, and go to the land of Moriah, and offer him there as a burnt offering upon one of the mountains of which I shall tell you." (Gen. 22:1–2)

How could God ask such a thing? For Abraham, to sacrifice Isaac was to sacrifice himself. It meant that Abraham would not live on, that the "people" would not be formed, that the blessing would die here and now. Yet this call was as clear as the first, and it was clearly the same God who was calling.

> So Abraham rose early in the morning, saddled his ass, and took two of his young men with him, and his son Isaac; and he cut the wood for the burnt offering, and arose and went to the place of which God had told him. . . . And Isaac said to his father Abraham, "My father!" And he said, "Here am I, my son." He said, "Behold, the fire and the wood; but where is the lamb for a burnt offering?" Abra-

ham said, "God will provide himself the lamb for a burnt
offering, my son." So they went both of them together."
(Gen. 22:3, 7–8)

Abraham loved God, and believed in him so deeply, that he was
able to respond to all that God asked of him. Because of this total
response to the call of the Lord, Abraham was blessed. The Lord
said to Abraham:

> By myself I have sworn, says the Lord, because you have
> done this, and have not withheld your son, your only son,
> I will indeed bless you, and I will multiply your descen-
> dants as the stars of heaven and as the sand which is on
> the seashore. (Gen. 22:16–17)

In the life of Jesus, the agony in Gethsemane was a point at
which the call of God was devastatingly clear. It was the wholehearted response that had to be arrived at. The Gospel accounts of
that struggle are often read in a matter-of-fact manner, as though
a few minutes of time spent "thinking the whole thing through"
were sufficient to resolve the dilemma. But listen to the words used
by one of the evangelists and hear the real agony that Jesus experienced:

> And taking with him Peter and the two sons of Zebedee, he
> began to be sorrowful and troubled. Then he said to them,
> "My soul is very sorrowful, even to death; remain here,
> and watch with me." And going a little farther he fell on
> his face and prayed, "My Father, if it be possible, let this
> cup pass from me; nevertheless, not as I will, but as you
> will." (Mt.26:37–39)

The peace that came to him, as the peace that came to Abraham,
found its source in the underlying conviction that, no matter what,
Jesus was being true to who he was; he was responding wholeheartedly—and in utmost honesty—to what he knew in his heart. In no
way could God forsake him; with his dying breath he could shout:

> I will tell of thy name to my brethren;
> in the midst of the congregation I will praise thee:
> You who fear the Lord, praise him!
> All you sons of Jacob, glorify him,

and stand in awe of him, and all you sons of Israel!
For he has not despised or abhorred
the affliction of the afflicted;
and he has not hid his face from him,
but has heard, when he cried to him.

Ps. 22:22–24

RESPONSE IN FREEDOM

That kind of faith—the faith of Abraham and the faith of Jesus—is a leap in the dark if ever there was one! The hearing, the daring to interpret that what was heard was from God, the responding to the point of giving up future and name and memory and life itself—all of this is so incredible!

These men were possessed! They, and so many women and men down through the ages, were so possessed by God and so taken up with deep love for him that nothing they themselves possessed made any difference. They were free—and their responses to the calls of the Lord in their lives were born of freedom. These great people of our history were able to walk this earth with nothing to lose. Everything they had, all that they were, was a gift from the giver of all good gifts. All could be returned without loss.

I have often wondered about the "stuff" out of which that freedom comes. There are so many factors in human experience that are threats to—indeed destroyers of—personal freedom. Some of these factors make of us free social beings. That is, the limitations are such that we can freely choose them so that we might be more loving, more responsive to others' needs, more capable of sharing in the work of liberation in our world. Other factors simply, sadly, make us unfree. They are neither freely chosen, nor liberating in any sense of the word. They alienate us from our brothers and sisters, from ourselves and from our God.

The problem is not that these factors, events, circumstances, come into our lives, but rather that the two kinds are often difficult to distinguish—at least, immediately. The temptations of Jesus at the beginning of his public ministry provide us with very good examples of this (Mt. 4:1–11; 1:12–13; Lk. 4:1–13).

Imagine, if you will, a person who is gradually coming to an awareness of power within himself, of a special call—to be and to do, for an entire people, someone and something that ultimately will be the criterion by which that people will judge the fidelity of God. And imagine the hopes of that people, whose history includes the glory of God-favored peoplehood and the pain and suffering of captivity and oppression and exile, whose history has known the exhilaration of victory in war and the devastation of defeat, whose history is one of encounter with a God of promises, and whose present is exhaustingly, depressingly, devoid of that once enjoyed (now only vicariously) brightness of power, and freedom, and the Lord's favor—a people that again (and still) walks in darkness.

If you can imagine that person and that people and that situation, then you can perhaps imagine the kinds of ambiguity and conflict that would be at play in the hearts of all who had so much at stake. However noble the motives, however sincere the persons, however numerous the signs, it would surely take a significant degree of "nerve" for anyone to claim to be the Messiah, and an even greater degree of "the stuff-of-freedom" to live out that mission in a way diametrically opposed to the popular beliefs and enthusiams about messiahship. Jesus was that person, and his response to the temptations gives us a good idea of what this "stuff-of-freedom" might be for us Christians.

The first temptation (recorded by Matthew) is the one to "command these stones (if you are the Son of God) to become loaves of bread" (Mt. 4:3). This was an invitation to Jesus to become "not-poor," not-dependent. It was a temptation to cease being who he was at his roots—Son, Word-made-flesh, one of the anawim. Satan seemed to be saying to Jesus that self-sufficiency would assure him a successful term of office as Messiah, and that a clever use of power would make the people happy and give them new hope. What made the difference for Jesus was his awareness of his own power. He knew, deep down, that he did not need magic for survival. And he did not delude himself into believing that independence was, in and of itself, an empowering virtue. Jesus was able to remain free to respond to God because he chose to be "gift-able." He must have known that his mission had more to do with relying on the Father than with having all he "needed" for success. He must have sensed that to receive all as gift allows the possibility of being free. So he was able to answer, "Man shall not live by bread alone, but by every word that proceeds from the mouth of God" (Mt. 4:4). In so saying, he grew in his freedom to respond to God's call.

Satan returned with a second temptation: "If you are the Son of God, throw yourself down" from the pinnacle of the temple (Mt. 4:6). This was a new invitation—to be not-humble, not-human, not-of-this-earth. Surely, such a show of God's favor would go a long way to building up a following! Again, this goes to the roots of who

Jesus is, and is a temptation to cease being what he is called to be: human—even in his need for the Father's love, over and above the love and respect of those to whom he was sent to minister. What made the difference here for Jesus was his awareness of God's love for him. He knew, deep down, that he did not need earthly glory for success. Jesus was able to remain free to respond to God because he chose to be "trusting." He must have known that his mission had more to do with hope in the Lord's promise than with the ability to "make God prove his love" in a sensational way. He must have known that deep trust in the Lord leads to deep freedom. And so he was able to answer, "It is written, 'You shall not tempt the Lord your God'" (Mt. 4:7). In so saying, he grew in his freedom to respond to God's call.

A third time Jesus was tempted: "All these (kingdoms of the world) I will give you, if you will fall down and worship me" (Mt. 4:9). The invitation is one to be not-obedient, not-singlehearted in his mission. After all, didn't he have the mission anyway of gathering to himself all of the kingdoms of the earth? But Jesus, at his roots, was not to be king so much as humble servant. What made the difference for Jesus at this point was that he was focusing on God's kingdom, which he was eager to seek first, above all else. He was able to remain free to respond to God because he chose to be "faithful." He must have known that his mission had more to do with fidelity to the Father than with the amassing of earthly, personal, shallow kingdoms. He must have known that singlehearted fidelity to God leads to a unique kind of freedom. And so he was able to say, "Begone, Satan! For it is written, 'You shall worship the Lord your God and him only shall you serve'" (Mt. 4:10). In so saying, he grew in his freedom to respond to God's call.

"Then the devil left him, and behold, angels came and ministered to him" (Mt. 4:11).

This incident in the life of Jesus speaks to many people, not so much because we find comfort in knowing that Jesus was temptable, but because the way in which he was tempted resonates with our own human experience. We humans generally find ourselves at our weakest—our most temptable—in matters that have to do with (a) our awareness of our own power as human beings (and the possibility of misusing that power or denying it altogether), (b) our awareness of God's boundless love for us (and the possibility of rejecting that love or losing hope in it), and (c) our focus on the kingdom of God (and the possibility of our losing that focus, "stepping out" of that kingdom, and establishing our own little kingdoms).

We are most susceptible to the deceits of the spirit of evil when we begin to see virtue in self-sufficiency, when our criteria for success are glory brought to ourselves and the esteem of all, when "being in control" and having our own kingdom becomes a sign of our "being together" and in touch with the Almighty.

True freedom to respond to the calls of the Lord in our lives comes from choices that we must make for ourselves. After the manner of Jesus, we must choose to be gift-able, trusting, and faithful. This means that we must—even as we minister to others—become willing to be ministered to. It means that we must—even as we live through doubt—become willing to let our knowledge of the Lord's love for us keep us from panic. And it means that we must—even as the illusion of power is placed before us—become willing to keep faith in our God who is Lord of all. Choosing to be gift-able, trusting and faithful will help us to identify with Christ who was poor and humble and obedient (Phil. 2). And this freedom will be integrated into our lives as a warm detachment from material goods, from esteem, from illusion.

In the last analysis, then, call remains a mystery. The ambiguity that surrounds vocation stays with us. For we must reach a point where we willingly, trustingly say, "I know that it is the Lord who is calling me, because my heart has heard my name. I know that the call is, at least, for me to become fully immersed in life. And I know that the Lord will bless this life—and me—because he is a God who is faithful." It is those people—like Jesus, like Abraham, like so many who have walked this earth—who are in touch with their own depth who finally claim the freedom to be children of God.

FAITH EXPERIENCE III

Faith Experience III involves prayer and sharing about our own experience of *call*. There is more time for personal prayer and reflection than in Faith Experiences I and II, especially because of the factors surrounding our being called by the Lord—the ambiguities, the doubts, the need for freedom—that we need to look at and pray about even as we engage in faith sharing. The role of the Tuner may be a more active one in this Faith Experience because of the nature of Sessions II and IV. These call for guided experiences of prayer, and require some preparation beforehand. In a sense, this Faith Experience begins where Faith Experience II left off, but does not require that those participating have taken part in the previous one. There are seven distinct sessions in Faith Experience III. As in the preceding one, participants should be asked to bring Bibles, or the Tuner should be sure to have some on hand for each person.

Session I

At the closing liturgy of Faith Experience II, the participants did some faith sharing about how they were able to love the Lord. The Scripture passage used as a basis for this sharing was the triple profession of love made by Peter in John 21. Faith Experience III begins at the same place, with the same Scripture passage, but this time with a particular focus on that love as a response to a call from the Lord.

This first session should begin in much the same way as the first two Faith Experiences begin. The participants should introduce themselves to one another (if necessary) and voice their expectations for the time they will spend together in faith sharing. The Tuner then comments briefly on the theme for this Faith Experience and reviews the basic ground rules for faith sharing (cf. Chapter 1). After that the Tuner gives a brief explanation of what will go on during the rest of this session, and sets the tone by reading the Scripture passage and calling the participants to ten or fifteen minutes of silent prayer and reflection on the question for sharing.

After the preliminaries described above, the group listens to John 21:1–17. The prayer, reflection and sharing to follow are based on the question: How (in the past three or four months—or since this group last was together for a Faith Experience) have I responded to the call of the Lord to love him? The Tuner should note that the question is a broad one that asks the participants to begin reflecting on whether they have been aware of calls from the Lord, and on how they have been able to respond to them. All should be encouraged, in their sharing, to be specific and concrete in the examples they give. These examples are experiences of faith that build up the community in the very sharing of them. The session should end with a period of shared prayer.

Session II

This session and the two that follow form parts of what we call the "Abraham-Isaac experience." They are a way of looking at the call of Abraham, at his faithfulness, and at the blessing of the Lord, while we look at what we have in our lives that enhances or takes away our own freedom for response. The basis for Sessions II, III, and IV will be sections from chapters 17–22 of Genesis. The purpose of Session II is to come to a clearer understanding of the abandonment and freedom that Abraham must have felt in giving himself totally to God, even in the midst of the confusion surrounding the calls he received.

The Tuner first sets a prayerful tone (best done by calling the group to a consciousness of the Lord's presence in their midst, and by a brief prayer) and invites the group to listen to the story of Abraham and Sarah and Isaac. This should be a slow, meditative reading of at least the following passages: Genesis 17:1–8, 15–21; 18:9–15; 21:1–8; and 22:1–18.

Once the reading is finished and the group has had a few minutes of silence to let the story sink in, they will get involved in a brief role-playing session in order to see, from different vantage points, the "gifting" that took place between Yahweh and Abraham and Sarah. This should not be an elaborate or complicated procedure, but one that will help the participants to retain a sense of the sacredness of that moment in salvation history. I suggest here two alternatives for this "role-playing."

The first is to split the large group into small groups of five or six and to be sure that one person takes the role of Abraham, one the role of Yahweh and one the role of Sarah. The others in the group might be servants of the family, or guests, or simply innocent bystanders hearing the story. Each small group would then try to gain some new insight into the experience of those people through their own re-enactment of those scenes.

A second way to accomplish this would be to have everyone stay in one large group and to take similar roles. In other words, it could be that four people would be Yahweh, four Abraham, four Sarah, and eight servants or bystanders. (It would be interesting to have a couple of those bystanders be twentieth-century people.) Instead of re-enacting the story they have just heard, however, the participants should be asked to spend fifteen minutes in reflection and to write out a statement (as though being issued by the person whose role they are playing) about the events that have taken place. These statements should reflect the mind and heart of the person (Abraham, Yahweh, Sarah, servant, bystander) and should have something to do with call and gift of self, with confusion or doubt, with laughter and promise, etc. Each one will then "issue" his or her statement (without discussion or comment) and the session will end with a brief prayer.

Session III

After a short break, the group is reassembled and a different kind of meditation takes place. This session is aimed at helping the participants to make personal application of the Abraham-Isaac experience. As mentioned earlier in this chapter, the call to Abraham to sacrifice Isaac was something that went to the heart of Abraham's very identity. Isaac was precious to him as a son, as the child of his old age, as a sign to him of God's power and faithfulness, and as the instrument itself—the means—through which God's promise was to be fulfilled and Abraham was to live on. What Abraham had come to value most in his life, he was now asked to sacrifice.

It is certainly true for us, too, that there are "things" in our lives that we come to value deeply, that become precious to us, and that, in a very real sense, become the way we identify ourselves. Whether these are factors basic to our identity (I am a man, a woman, a Christian, a child of God), or people in our lives (I am a wife, a husband, a child, a parent), or personal gifts and talents (I am a chemist, a pianist, a good organizer, a Ph.D. in clinical psychology), or possessions of other kinds (I am the proud owner of this mansion, I am blond and green-eyed, I am thirty-three years old, I am the president of this company), they are all, in their own way, "Isaacs" in our lives. They might be ways through which God fulfills his promises to us, or precious possessions that we are called to sacrifice, or both. At any rate, they must be *gift* from the Lord—or we cease being gift-able.

In Session III, the Tuner (or someone from the group) once again reads Genesis 22:1–18. The remainder of the session is a time of silence during which the participants are asked to write down ten "Isaacs" in their lives—the people, gifts, and parts of themselves that they value most. (It would be helpful here if the Tuner had a stack of small pieces of paper—ten for each participant. It is important for what will follow that each of the "Isaacs" be written on a separate piece of paper.) The ten are then stacked up in order of priority, from least to greatest, with the least valued on the top and the most valued on the bottom.

In a period of personal prayer (all should be encouraged to go off to a place where they can be alone) each participant is asked to give up the "Isaacs" in his or her life. The Tuner might suggest that the participants consider each "Isaac" individually, set the paper aside as a symbol of giving up, and in the presence of the Lord experience the loss of that "possession." What must be stressed in this kind of prayer is the doing of it before the Lord. For even when we have given up everything, sacrificed all, we still are possessed by a God who loves us. And we stand free—more apt to hear God calling to us and more likely to be able to respond wholeheartedly.

Session IV

Session IV is the conclusion of the Abraham-Isaac experience. After experiencing the loss of sacrifice, we must experience being gifted by the Lord. This is, in fact, the second part of the prayer begun in the previous session. It is recommended that each person read Genesis 22:1–18 individually, and pray alone, but that this time they all take back their "Isaacs"—receiving each one of them as gifts from God—and spending some time experiencing the "giftness" of it all. It is possible, after all, to remain free even with the many gifts that are ours through the great goodness of our God. It is perhaps even possible to have "warm detachment" from everything created and given to us only when we can sacrifice all and receive all as gift. And it is with this kind of freedom that comes from this sacrificing all (this making all things sacred) that we can more clearly hear and more fully respond to whatever the Lord calls us.

This "stuff of our freedom" is also the "stuff of our faith," and is worthy to be shared. And so, Session IV ends with a period of faith sharing. At this time, in groups of seven or eight (see Chapter 1, note 13), the participants are asked to share: (a) some of the things they chose as "Isaacs" and why, (b) how they felt as they were giving up and receiving as gift, (c) where God seemed to be in all of this, and (d) how they feel now. It is likely that the group will want to spend a bit of time in shared prayer to bring this session to a close.

Session V

Often we don't understand or appreciate what is true in our lives until we have had a chance to think about and to relate to others specific instances of those truths. It is not uncommon for those who take part in Faith Experience I, for example, to come away delighted, but amazed, by the realization that they had even had faith experiences—real experiences of a real God alive and active in their own lives and activities. Going out of our way to identify such specific instances of calls, and sharing those with the people around us, is the purpose of Session V.

In setting the tone for this session, the Tuner should say a few extra words about the nature of this sharing. Perhaps using examples of calls from Scripture would help to illustrate the point to be made. And the point is this: that in human history the only discernible pattern considered by God in calling whomever he calls seems to be that God touches the uniqueness of each individual. When God calls, he does not say, "See how I called this person, or that one: this is how I am calling you now." Rather, the message seems to be: "My child, do you see how you are unique in all of the world? I am, therefore, calling you as I have never called anyone." Apparently, the way God calls us is as singular, as unmatched, as our own names. While it is true that others may have the same names as we do, when our own name is called it has a ring to it that is unmistakable to us. And it calls forth all that is special and unique about us.

Very often, the vibrancy of the Christian community depends on our ability to recognize and respect the uniqueness of each person's call from the Lord. We must learn to hear our own names, and to help our brothers and sisters to hear theirs. This must be true, also, for wives and husbands, for children in a family, and for members of religious communities. Growth together takes place only when individual growth is allowed and fostered—only when the uniqueness of each individual is welcomed as the source of the richness of the whole community.

It may be that we will experience a reluctance to talk about the calls of the Lord in our lives. After all, we never really know for sure that we have been called, or that it was the Lord calling. Nor are we always eager to proclaim from the rooftops the reluctance of our response or the less-than-perfect quality of that "Here I am, Lord!" Nor is it all that easy to talk about ambiguity and ambivalence and confusion. Nor does it appear to be all that humble to acknowledge that the Lord has indeed touched our lives, called us, and that we have indeed responded. Session V gives us an opportunity to do this kind of sharing.

The Tuner may wish to use one of the following Scripture passages to begin the session (or to begin a brief period of prayer after the introductory remarks):

Genesis 17:1–8   Exodus 3:1–12
1 Samuel 3:1–11   1 Samuel 16:6–13

Isaiah 6:1–13   Jeremiah 1:4–10
Luke 1:26–38   Matthew 4:18–22
Acts 9:1–19

After about fifteen minutes of prayer and reflection, sharing takes place on the questions: How do I feel God is calling me? (or: What are the calls from God that I experience in my life?) What is it that makes me feel called by the Lord? It may be that people will talk about their vocation in life, or they may wish to focus on those "daily" calls from the Lord. The Tuner should make it clear that it is entirely up to the participants to determine what they will share with the group.

Session VI

The more we get in touch with *call* in our lives, the more likely is it that we will grow in our awareness of our doubts and our fears and our refusals to accept those calls. We all have our own limitations, and the recognition of those limitations is important if we are to sharpen our ability and our freedom to respond. Often it is our holding on to those doubts—without naming them, without acknowledging them—that keeps us closed to the possibility of new modes of response. In a sense, we enslave ourselves by refusing to let go of our fears, our uncertainties—sometimes our cynicism—about our God and about the strange and difficult and frightening depths to which he calls us.

In Session VI, the participants will spend some time reflecting on the doubts they experience and will pray together in thanksgiving to a God who holds out a promise of freedom and life to those who follow him—and who keeps his promise. This second part, the prayer together, is intended to be a eucharistic celebration. The first part, reflection and sharing about doubt, could easily be done as part of the liturgy of the word. There are several Scripture passages which reflect this aspect of call. Particularly apt would be the temptations of Jesus, Gethsemane, or the call of Jeremiah.

It may be that the group will also wish to have a celebration of reconciliation during this liturgy as a way of "letting go" of our limitations and recognizing the Lordship of Jesus the liberator. Hosea 14 is the articulation of a call that is one of reconciliation, of total acceptance from the Lord.

However this session is put together by the Tuner (and the

group), it should include: (a) time for personal prayer and reflection on doubts and on the Lord's promises as we experience these, (b) time for sharing the fruit of our prayer, and (c) a eucharistic celebration.

Session VII

The final session of Faith Experience III has three parts: a meditation, a sharing session, and a closing Eucharist. The first part is a guided meditation based on Chapter 2 of the Acts of the Apostles. It is intended to be a prayer through which the Tuner will focus the community on the Spirit of Christ—that Spirit which animates us and helps us to hear and to respond to our God. During this prayer, the group is asked to consider the disciples of Jesus before the coming of the Holy Spirit, and to look at them after the Pentecost event. They were then a different group of people indeed—people with a new freedom, with new courage, with a new way of responding to life within them, people who could, like Peter, proclaim a new way of living:

> Repent, and be baptized every one of you in the name of Jesus Christ for the forgiveness of your sins; and you shall receive the gift of the Holy Spirit. For the promise is to you and to your children and to all that are far off, every one whom the Lord our God calls to him. (Acts 2:38–39)

This meditation should include a prayerful reading of Acts 2 and some input (meditative) from the Tuner.

At the end of the meditation, the Tuner proposes fifteen minutes of silence before the sharing. The questions, for the reflection and the sharing, are: What is the Lord asking of me now? What do I ask of him in order to be better able to respond? In one sense this will be the most difficult of the sharing sessions, because it calls for a verbalization of something that goes to our very depth and that implies some kind of commitment to response. It is also a sharing that leads us to acknowledge our need for the Lord's help—perhaps through this group of people with whom we are sharing. Many times, the call and the need are really two sides of the same coin. It is both call and need that bring us closer to the Lord, and it is both that we bring to the Eucharist, in thanksgiving and in petition. (One possibility for this sharing is to ask the participants to make a kind of "badge" on which they would write the call and the need, and which they would wear during the liturgy. This would be helpful for the closing part of the celebration.)

The liturgy should be a simple one, based on the Lord's promise to send us the Spirit to help us hear and understand the truth in our lives (Jn. 16:1–15). As in Faith Experience I we had the Christ seal, and in Faith Experience II we had a blessing and missioning ceremony, so now, in Faith Experience III, we have a way of responding to those with whom we have been sharing our faith about call. This can be referred to as a "circle of prayer and blessing." We offer here two different ways in which this can be done.

One way would be to use the prayer of the faithful after the liturgy of the word as a time during which the participants will confirm the calls and pray for the needs that have been expressed. Each person, for example, could be assigned one member of the group whose call that person would affirm in prayer and whose needs he or she would pray for. This means that each one would pray aloud for one other person, and that all would have been brought before the Lord in prayer.

The second way would be to invite each one to speak to and pray for every other person in the group, perhaps just before the final blessing. The procedure to be followed would be similar to the rite of peace or the "blessing and missioning ceremony" described in Session VII of Faith Experience II.

So ends Faith Experience III. Somehow when we share at this level, it becomes clearer that we are indeed connected, to one another, even in our uniqueness. The calls of the Lord can often be heard, and doubts and fears can be overcome, only when we realize that we are special and that freedom is a gift that can be ours. A Christian community—a group of people willing to share their experience of a God who calls—makes that freedom and that hearing all the more possible.

The following is a synopsis of Faith Experience III (Call) as it fits into a weekend schedule.

SESSION I

Friday Evening—7:30–9:00

(a) The Tuner gives a short introduction to faith sharing and sets down some basic guidelines for the weekend.
(b) The Tuner then sets the tone for the first exercise.

(c) Initial Sharing: (1) The Tuner reads John 21:1–17. (2) Fifteen minutes of personal prayer and reflection on the question, "How (in the past three or four months—or since this group last was together for a Faith Experience) have I responded to the call of the Lord to love him?" (3) Sharing on this question. (4) Shared prayer.

SESSION II

Saturday Morning—9:00–11:00

(a) Brief prayer of presence before the Lord.
(b) Slow meditative reading of the story of Abraham and Sarah and Isaac: Gen. 17:1–8, 15–21; 18:9–15; 21:1–8; 22:1–18.
(c) Role play of this story. This can be done in small groups or in one large group. See explanation in this chapter.
(d) End with a brief prayer.

SESSION III

Saturday Morning—11:15–12:15

(a) The Tuner once again reads Genesis 22:1–18.
(b) The participants write down ten "Isaacs" in their lives—the people, gifts, and parts of themselves that they value most. Each "Isaac" should be written on a separate piece of paper and stacked up in order of priority, from the least to the greatest, with the least valued on top and the most valued on the bottom.
(c) Personal prayer time during which each gives up the "Isaacs" in his or her life. Participants should be encouraged to set the papers aside one by one in a symbolic act of surrender, and to experience—*in the Lord's presence*—the loss of that "possession."

SESSION IV

Saturday Afternoon—2:00–4:00

(a) A continuation of the personal prayer begun in the previous session. Each individual should reread the Genesis passage and then take back the "Isaacs"—receiving each one of them as gifts from God, and spending some time experiencing the "gift-ness" of it all.

(b) The last hour of this session is a period of faith sharing in small groups on: (1) some of the things I chose as "Isaacs" and why, (2) how I felt as I was giving them up and receiving them as gift, (3) where God seemed to be in all of this, and (4) how I feel now.

SESSION V

Saturday Afternoon—4:30–5:30

(a) The Tuner sets the tone for this session by reading a passage from Scripture. See list of suggestions given earlier in this chapter.

(b) Fifteen minutes of silent prayer and reflection.

(c) Faith sharing on the questions: (1) How do I feel God is calling me? (or What are the calls from God that I experience in my life?) (2) What is it that makes me feel called by the Lord?

SESSION VI

Saturday Evening—7:30–9:00

(a) The Tuner sets the tone for this session (by reading, e.g., Mt. 4:1–11 or Jer. 1:4–10) and explains what sharing will take place.

(b) Fifteen minutes of personal prayer and reflection.

(c) Faith sharing on: (1) How do I experience doubt in my life? (2) What do I hear to be the Lord's promise(s) to me? (The group may also want to include a celebration of reconciliation at this time.)

(d) Eucharistic celebration.

SESSION VII

Sunday Morning—9:00–12:00

(a) Guided prayer/meditation on Acts 2: the Spirit of Christ animates us and helps us to hear and respond to our God.

(b) Fifteen minutes of silent prayer and reflection.

(c) Faith sharing on the questions: (1) What is the Lord asking of me now? (2) What do I ask of him in order to be better able to respond?

(d) A closing liturgy, based on John 16:1–15, and including a "circle of prayer and blessing."

4 — Faith Experience IV
THE BEATITUDES

Blessed are the poor in spirit, for theirs is the kingdom of heaven.

Blessed are those who mourn, for they shall be comforted.

Blessed are the meek, for they shall inherit the earth.

Blessed are those who hunger and thirst for righteousness, for they shall be satisfied.

Blessed are the merciful, for they shall obtain mercy.

Blessed are the pure in heart, for they shall see God.

Blessed are the peacemakers, for they shall be called sons of God.

Blessed are those who are persecuted for righteousness' sake, for theirs is the kingdom of heaven.

Mt. 5:3–10

Jesus was an amazing sort of human being. He lived among his people in a way that was strikingly different. The message he preached, the things he did, the friends he gathered around himself, the people he challenged, those he criticized, the way he prayed, the way he suffered and died—all of these things tell us something about who this man was. But even more amazing, these things are supposed to be able to give us some idea about who *we* are called, by that man, to become.

When Jesus sent his Spirit to the apostles and to his Church at Pentecost, he was saying more than: "Here is your protector and counselor. Be brave, and bold; understand now all that I told you when I was with you." And at the Last Supper, when Jesus left to his apostles and to his Church his body and blood in the Eucharist, he was saying more than: "Be nourished, my friends, and reminded and reassured that I am with you." And when Jesus proclaimed the Beatitudes, he was saying more than: "Be patient, my people, because there is a place beyond, where the way you live now and what you suffer now will be the cause of your happiness later."

Surely he was saying all of those things to his followers. But there seems to have been a different kind of urgency in those words, and in many others which he spoke. It was the urgency of someone whose mission needed to be continued by people whose lives would be constant reminders to the world—whose very lives, in fact, would be proof—that he was alive and the source of life, that the mission was a success, that the world had been given new life, new hope, new cause for rejoicing and giving thanks. And so there was more in those words. There was command and plea: "Live in my Spirit! Let *your* body be broken and *your* blood be poured out for the life of the world! Know the blessing of living by those values by which I have lived my life, and experience real happiness!" There was command and plea in those words: "Be like me, because those in your world should get a chance to see me, too, and because who-ever has seen me has been able to catch a glimpse of God. And happy is that person!"

When Jesus proclaimed the Beatitudes, he was describing him-self: he was letting people know something about his values, his struggles, his sufferings and his joys. At the same time, he was promising them a share in his joy if they would share the rest. In a sense, Jesus was inviting us to see, first-hand, how his humanity and his relationship to the universe were occasions for God's bless-ing. The Beatitudes then become not empty or theoretical promises, but promises born out of the conviction of personal, human expe-rience. We, too, are heirs of those promises. Let us look at the Be-atitudes in that light.

BLESSED ARE THE POOR IN SPIRIT ...

Those of us who have been brought up with the traditions of Christianity relating to the birth of Jesus have also, even if only in the back of our minds, grown up believing that Jesus was poor—born in a manger, no room at the inn, son of a lowly carpenter. And we have probably grown comfortable with the idea. He never seemed to lack anything. He didn't need much anyway. And he did, after all, choose poverty.

The problem arises when we begin hearing Jesus, time and again, call his followers to make the same choice for themselves. He is calling us to choose poverty! Then it becomes necessary to ask se-rious questions about who Jesus was, and how he lived his life, and what exactly he might be calling us to. We have been taught all along that poverty was a special calling, to special people—those who follow the evangelical counsels. But in the Beatitudes, there seems to be a call that transcends even the counsels. In the Beatitudes Jesus tells his people—all of them—that his real happiness comes from being poor in spirit. And he tells them that they, too, have a right to that happiness, that blessing.

If we look at the Beatitudes as the primary values by which Jesus was motivated and which characterized his ministry, then this first one—being poor in spirit—can easily be seen as the key, as that one factor in his life that freed him to wholeheartedly give himself as ransom for the whole world. It was that poverty of spirit—reflected in his life through all the Gospels—that made it possible for him to be faithful, to be Son, to empty himself (Phil. 2:1–11), to die for us, to possess the kingdom of God.

This poverty, however, and this spirit which animated Jesus extended beyond the fact that he was born poor. There are things Jesus gave up and things he suffered and things he chose that constituted real poverty of spirit and that we must consider in responding to Jesus' command and plea that we live in his Spirit.

The Gospels tell us much about the poverty of Jesus. We can read that he gave up family and home for the sake of the kingdom (Mk. 3:31–35; Mt. 8:19). He gave up his privacy (Mk. 1:35; 6:31; 7:24) and status (Mk. 12:13–14) and ultimately his own will (Mt. 26:39) and his life (Lk. 23:46). And there were elements in his life that he might not have chosen for himself but that he had to suffer at the hands of the people around him—friend and foe alike. Jesus suffered misunderstanding (Mk. 5:14–17), betrayal (Jn. 18:15), abandonment (Mt. 26:56), and dishonor (Lk 4:16–30). At the same time, he chose to be servant of all (Jn. 13:1–20) and the least among them (Mk. 12:13–14). He chose to be broken to give wholeness to all, and to be the body and blood that would provide nourishment and strength to all.

Through all of this, Jesus gave poverty many different meanings, and he gave the spirit of poverty a special significance—not just for those who follow the "evangelical counsels," but for all, and not just a token nod to those who are in want, but a real identification with the anawim of God, with those who enjoy the special favor of God, with the poor. Jesus could not simply have been giving an encouraging word to the poor around him when he said, "Blessed are the poor in spirit. . . ." That would have been condescending and callous. He had to be saying something about himself, about how he knew blessing in his life because he knew poverty. He had to be saying something like: "It is through the things given up, the suffering endured, and the choices made that I have come to know the real, deep, lasting, effective freedom that lets me seek first the kingdom of God. That makes me very happy; it makes me blessed. And you who live by that same spirit—you, too, are blessed."

It is really necessary, when considering these aspects of the life and ministry of Jesus, to try to feel for ourselves what Jesus might have felt. We must try to get inside his spirit if we are to let that spirit animate us. And this seems most difficult to do with respect to poverty of spirit. I suspect we have learned to take for granted the depth of feeling that Jesus showed in his life, or even to explain it away as something else. But consider, if you will: How could a man who loved children as Jesus did (Mk. 10:13–16), and who understood love within a family as he did (Lk. 15:11–32), not feel deeply his own poverty—however freely chosen, however clearly a response to his Father—when he said things like: "Who are my mother and my brother and my sisters?" (Mk. 3:31–35) or "The Son of Man has nowhere to lay his head" (Mt. 8:20)?

How could a man who sought to be with his God (Mk. 1:35) and who was pleading for people to believe in him and in his Father on the basis of his person and words rather than because of miracles (Jn. 6:25–29)—how could such a man not experience the loss of his privacy or the poverty of being misunderstood? How could a man who felt so strongly about his friends—and who himself was so loyal as a friend (Jn. 15:12–17)—not feel deeply the pain and loss of betrayal, and denial, and abandonment by those closest to him? How could someone who did so much good not experience real poverty when asked to leave a place where he had done a frighteningly good thing (Mk. 5:14–17) or when threatened by his own townspeople because they figured that it was impossible for him to be who he claimed he was?

The man had feelings! The sense of loss, of poverty, was part of his life. Some of it he chose; some was forced upon him by those who knew not what they did. All of it was accepted ungrudgingly. All of it was part of the growth of Jesus in the spirit of poverty. All of it had to do with his growth in freedom. All of it was a source of blessing for him.

Our lives are filled with experiences of poverty. Our world is filled with poverty at so many levels, and we try to fight that poverty at the same time that we proclaim it as a requisite for blessedness. Small wonder that we do so badly in either direction! It is the spirit of Jesus, poor and humble, that must animate us. That spirit, I believe, is one which leads us to an ungrudging acceptance of whatever poverty comes to us. It is a spirit that helps us to recognize those feelings in our brothers and sisters throughout the world, and that impels us to *choose* to be with the poorest among us, to be—with Jesus—the servant of all, and the least among all, willing to be broken and to give up body and life's blood that others might live.

That spirit of poverty is one which Jesus tried to illustrate for his followers throughout his preaching ministry:

> Do not lay up for yourselves treasures on earth, where moth and rust consume and where thieves break in and steal. (Mt. 6:19)

> Therefore, I tell you, do not be anxious about your life, what you shall eat, nor about your body, what you shall put on. (Lk. 12:22)

> You received without paying; give without pay. Take no gold, nor silver, nor copper in your belts, no bag for your journey. (Mt. 10:5–15)

> The kingdom of heaven is like a treasure hidden in a field, which a man found and covered up; then in his joy he goes and sells all that he has and buys that field. (Mt. 13:44)

> If any man would come after me, let him deny himself and take up his cross and follow me. For whoever would save his life will lose it, and whoever loses his life for my sake will find it. For what will it profit a man, if he gains the whole world and forfeits his life? (Mt. 16:24–26)

> You lack one thing; go, sell what you have, and give to the poor, and you will have treasure in heaven; and come, follow me. (Mk. 10:17–22)

> Truly I tell you, this poor widow has put in more than all of them; for they all contributed out of their abundance, but she out of her poverty put in all the living that she had. (Lk. 21:1–4).

That spirit of poverty is what enabled Jesus, and what can enable us, to walk this earth in meekness and making peace, merciful toward all, able to mourn, hungry and thirsty for justice, willing to accept persecution for the sake of justice, singlehearted in the desire to be faithful to God. He was able to walk this earth with nothing to lose, and he gained everything. The kingdom of God was his. And he is blessed—happy—for all time. Blessed, indeed, are the poor in spirit, for theirs is the kingdom of God.

BLESSED ARE THEY WHO MOURN . . .

Mourning is not an easy thing. It seems rather to be a painful human emotion—one that yields only sadness, one that often seeks a situation or a person or an event to blame for the hurt that is experienced. How can mourning and blessing even be used in the same sentence? How is it conceivable that those who mourn are, in fact, blessed?

In Luke's version of the Beatitudes (Lk. 6:17, 20–23), the dilemma is resolvable. Those who weep now are blessed with the promise of a future time when they will be able to laugh. Those who live in the sadness of poverty, oppression, death, and evil in the world will one day live in the gladness of the fulfilled promise of a loving God. Good will overcome evil. Justice will be done. Life itself will have overcome all death. Those people hear the revelation of "a new heaven and a new earth" where God himself will be with his own and will "wipe away every tear from their eyes, and death shall be no more, neither shall there be mourning, nor crying nor pain anymore" (Rev. 21:1–4).

If Jesus was describing himself, however, then he was referring to himself as one who mourned now, and as one blessed now. Blessing came because of the mourning, not in spite of it. And so, mourning takes on a new meaning and the Beatitude becomes one that is applicable even to those among us who do not consider ourselves mourners. The value expressed and lived by Jesus is one that he calls us to live by.

Mostly, Jesus mourned—as the Scriptures tell us—when human life was destroyed, when human dignity was denied, or when humanity itself rejected the healing of its God. And Jesus mourned because of his own pain and suffering. Luke records the time when Jesus rebuked the lawyers:

> Woe to you lawyers also! for you load men with burdens
> hard to bear, and you yourselves do not touch the burdens
> with one of your fingers. (Lk. 11:46)

He was mourning for his people, because he saw their dignity as human beings who were being trampled upon. At other times, Jesus mourned the loss of his friend Lazarus (Jn. 11) and wept over the city of Jerusalem:

> O Jerusalem, Jerusalem, killing the prophets and stoning
> those who are sent to you! How often would I have gathered your children together as a hen gathers her brood under her wings, and you would not! (Mt. 23:37)

Jesus felt strongly the pain and hurt of those who were blind and lame, of those possessed by unclean spirits, of lepers and of the outcasts of society (Mk. 1:32–34), even of weary travelers who followed him all day long without food for their stomachs, so strong was their hunger for the words he spoke (Lk. 9:11–17). And he knew his own pain and was able to mourn even on his own account (Mk. 14:32–35).

From the time we are little children, society teaches us that it is not very "grown-up" to cry. It is a sign of weakness. And yet, we have so much to mourn in our lives and in our world. Perhaps the real blessing of this second Beatitude is the blessing of joining our hearts to the heart of a God who knew that mourning kept one from being hardened to the reality of the destruction of human dignity, a God who knew that being able to suffer with those who suffered did not mean becoming a sad person.

Our world experiences death daily. And there must be those who are willing to support the world in its pain and hurt. There must be people who are willing to feel, with the world, the loss of those countless millions who starve to death, the agony of those human beings who are tortured and dehumanized in political prisons, the frustration of those whose human rights are denied, the tragedy of lives ended before birth, the sadness of those neglected and set aside because age has rendered them "useless" to society. The world needs people who can say to it, "I love you so much that I don't want you to hurt anymore. I don't want you to die. And I sincerely mourn the death you experience."

Christ calls us to be that people. Christianity must be a way of living that includes a willingness to mourn. Those who can mourn will not be so caught up in determining where to lay the blame that they will find themselves unable to bring comfort to those who hurt. Those who mourn will rather find themselves to be a people of gentle heart who will receive God's special comfort and strength and who will know now, in this broken world, the healing touch of God. That is the promise. Blessed are they who mourn, for they shall be comforted.

BLESSED ARE THE MEEK ...

It has become almost trite to say, "God's ways are not our ways." It is the kind of saying that everybody believes—as a saying. But the truth of it does not necessarily become part of the way we live. Rather, this situation—the fact that God's ways are different from ours—becomes an excuse for the mistakes we make or takes the form of a "communal shrug-of-the-shoulder" when we realize that "our ways," sadly, cost lives or keep people in poverty or walk over the weaklings of society. "After all, we're only human, and, besides, it's probably better that only a few have death dealt to them than that power get into the hands of the wrong people."

The Beatitude about meekness is a statement about power—and the values it proclaims are gentleness, sensitivity, humility, and non-violence. There are many instances in the Gospels where it becomes clear that Jesus lived by those values. And it is clear, too, that those values were important because they stood as countersigns to all that was death-dealing to the people of his day. Those who were oppressed in those days suffered at the hands of the scribes and the Pharisees who "lorded it over them" (Mt. 23), of lawyers who piled up burdens on them (Lk. 11:46), and of tax collectors who often cheated them (Lk. 19:1–10). They were even occasionally at each other's throats in a struggle for power (Mk. 10:35–45). Jesus recognized how all of this was sapping the strength and energy of his people, making them less happy, and so much of his teaching and example was focused on this question of power. "Come to me," he said, "all who labor and are heavy laden, and I will give you rest. Take my yoke upon you, and learn from me; for I am gentle and lowly in heart" (Mt. 11:25–28).

For Jesus, meekness included gentleness and was manifested in many ways during the years of his ministry. He could be approached by children, and have them close to him, and touch them with his blessing (Mt. 19:13–15). The children themselves must have sensed that here was a gentle man. Jesus gently touched with healing those who were sick or possessed by evil spirits and assured them that, of course, he wanted them to see, or walk, or be cleansed (Mk. 1:40–42). The lives of sinners were touched with the gentleness of Jesus: "Has no one condemned you?" (Jn. 8:1–11). This was all in striking contrast to the people around him who did not seem to want to be bothered by the children, who presumed that illness was God's way of punishing those who had the misfortune of being sinners, who rejected sinners and would kill them in the name of God.

This meekness in Jesus gave him sensitivity to the sufferings of those who experienced the hurt of death (Lk. 7:11–17), or of illness (Lk. 13:10–13), or of hunger (Mt. 14:13–21), or of their own sinfulness (Jn. 5:13–14). It gave him a humility through which he could befriend the earth and nature (Mk. 4:35–41), and through which he could teach the real limits of true friendship (Jn. 13). And it gave him a sense of God-given power, the non-violent power that seeks neither to judge nor to get revenge (Mt. 5:38–42), that proclaims peace rather than the sword (Mt. 26:52), and that permits a sacrifice of self that is freely chosen and, therefore, effective in bringing about salvation to the world (Jn. 10:17–18).

Meekness is hardly the sought-for characteristic of today's world. The issue is still power and the question is still who will own/control the earth. And the power struggle continues to work itself out at all levels of life. We continue killing each other in the name of peace; we continue stepping over each other to advance in our work; we continue lying to each other because "it is often the only way to protect the truth"; we continue destroying creation in the name of progress; we continue spending billions of dollars on armaments to be able to protect those millions of people who are too weak from starvation to protect their own interests; we continue aborting human life in the name of freedom.

Our heroes are Superman and Wonder Woman; our goals are wealth, possessions, status, "an edge over the next person," because we have become convinced that strength and power are measured according to the degree to which we are able to destroy another person or another business, another ideology or another government. This is diametrically opposed to the values lived by the Lord of life; the Christian message is that the meek will inherit the earth. It is those who follow Jesus in his gentleness, in his care and concern for all people and for all of creation, in his non-violence, in his willingness to belong to the earth (humility), who will experience real power. They will know the blessing of being heirs of the kingdom of Christ. Blessed are the meek, for they shall inherit the earth.

BLESSED ARE THOSE WHO HUNGER
AND THIRST FOR RIGHTEOUSNESS ...

When we were created, we were established in relationships. Our very situation related us to God, to the world, to all other persons, and to ourselves. I believe that justice, in its simplest and most profound sense, means the right ordering of those relationships. Certainly the justice of God in Scripture is seen as his fidelity to the personal covenant relationship which he established with his people, and which was renewed in the blood of Jesus. The Just God is the one who remained God to his people and the one who kept calling his people to be his people. Practically speaking, those on earth who are the victims of injustice are those who suffer because the relationships into which they have been created are in disorder. To realize the disorder and to work to set things right seems to be the point of this fourth Beatitude. The value being proclaimed is the "global relatedness" of all creation.

Jesus called God "Abba" and claimed that his food was to do the will of the one who sent him (Jn. 4:34). His fidelity to that relationship brought God's favor and revelation and constant presence to him. Jesus knew that he was blessed. He loved the *earth* and cherished his relationship to it. He trusted ultimately that the dominion over the earth given to human beings was real and had something to do with our faith (Mt. 17:20–21). And he was vindicated in his own belief, and was blessed in his "interaction" with nature (Mk. 6:45–52). In his relationships with *others,* Jesus was teacher, nourisher, healer, reconciler, friend, etc. He valued the people around him and sought to be at peace with everyone and to give all their due. He showed respect even for those who were looked down upon by others—tax collectors and sinners, Gentiles, Samaritans, women, etc. And Jesus believed in *himself,* trusted what was deep within him, and never lost sight of God's tremendous love for him.

As Jesus lived, so did he teach. He spent his life trying to teach those around him all he could about how they stood in relationship to God, to their world, to each other (and all others), and to themselves. His hunger and thirst for justice were strong and constant motivating forces for what he said and did. He proclaimed a God who was "Abba"—*a gentle and loving Father*—even for them (Mt. 6:7–15). Jesus taught about a *world that was gift* rather than enemy, a world whose beauties were themselves teachers about the great goodness of God (Lk. 12:22–31), a world which was a good enough place to be the very dwelling place of God (Jn. 1:14). He constantly challenged those who followed him (whether out of love or curiosity or hatred) to recognize that *the lives of all were precious,* and that each had a responsibility to the next person because each was called to be a neighbor to all (Lk. 10:29–37). And Jesus gently called people to believe in themselves (Lk. 17:20–21), *to be gentle with themselves,* and to trust that God's love for them was personal and unique to each (Jn. 10:1–18).

We, in our day, in our world, live in the same relationships. And the challenge of Jesus' teaching remains for us. We are called to live a belief that the right ordering of those relationships will be effective in bringing about justice in our world. That is the blessing promised by Jesus. Part of our problem is that we do not always recognize our own participation in injustice. In a sense, we need someone to focus us on the "food" so that we will realize that we hunger.

This is not a suggestion that we promote unhappiness, or "guilt trips." It is simply a suggestion that we look seriously at how that value lived by Jesus is operative in our lives. Is our God, for example, a nasty sort of "vigilante" whose real function is the destruction of those who make mistakes in life? Is that God one who wants us to live in constant fear of misreading what his will for us might be? Or is our God a real, loving, gentle, personal God who especially wants us to be with him? Do we attend to this relationship with God, much as we would attend to a love relationship with another person?

Do we receive the world—all of creation—as gift? And do we take care of that gift? Or are we squanderers of our world—wasting its resources, hoarding its goods, careless about its future? Do we use the things of creation for the good of humanity or for its destruction? Are we at peace with our earth?

Is our relatedness to other human beings selective? Or do we see ourselves as part of *one human family?* Are we building up a sensitivity to the hearts of those who are far away from us, or are we letting physical distance constitute a wall that will leave us comfortable in our not-knowing? Are there some people on this earth whose death, or starvation, or oppression we can learn to tolerate? Or as St. Paul put it:

> As it is, there are many parts, yet one body. The eye cannot say to the hand, "I have no need of you," nor again the head to the feet, "I have no need of you." . . . If one member

suffers, all suffer together; if one member is honored, all rejoice together. (1 Cor. 12:20–26)

Do we believe this, or have we learned not to suffer when one member suffers, and not to rejoice when one is honored?

Finally, do we work at fostering a relationship with ourselves? Do we love ourselves enough to love others and trust ourselves enough to trust others? Do we give ourselves time just to be with ourselves, to communicate, to be intimate, so that we can be self-possessed enough to give ourselves to others in life-giving intimacy?

The promise of Jesus—the blessing of this Beatitude—is that if we let ourselves hunger and thirst for justice, for the right ordering of our relationships, we will experience that for which we hunger and thirst. The more attuned we are to the possibilities that come from our close connectedness to God, to the world, to all other human beings, and to ourselves, the more those possibilities are transformed into reality in our lives. Blessed are those who hunger and thirst for justice, for they shall be satisfied.

BLESSED ARE THE MERCIFUL . . .

The mercy of Jesus is probably best exemplified in his willingness to let power go out of him for the benefit of others:

As he went, the people pressed round him. And a woman who had had a flow of blood for twelve years and could not be healed by anyone came up behind him and touched the fringe of his garment; and immediately her flow of blood ceased. And Jesus said, "Who was it that touched me?" When all denied it, Peter said, "Master, the multitudes surround you and press upon you!" But Jesus said, "Someone touched me; for I perceive that power has gone forth from me." And when the woman saw that she was not hidden, she came trembling, and falling down before him declared in the presence of all the people why she had touched him, and how she had been immediately healed. And he said to her, "Daughter, your faith has made you well; go in peace." (Lk. 8:42–48)

While it is important for us to be willing to touch others—and certainly Jesus touched those he healed (Mt. 20:34)—it is perhaps even more important to let others touch us. It is when we let the hurt of others touch us deeply that we are truly able to be merciful.

How often do we read in the Gospels about Jesus being moved to compassion for his people (Mt. 14:14)? He was a human being who was open to what was in the hearts of others (Mt. 19:16–22), who could share in their suffering (Mk. 7:31–37), and in their rejoicing (Jn. 2:1–11), and who could be drawn by their greatest needs. He was gentle without being compromising (Jn. 4), forgiving without being judgmental (Jn. 8). He knew what real power was (Mt. 21:21–22) and chose to use it only to touch people's hearts (Mt. 15:29–31; 16:1–4).

Many times in his ministry, Jesus was merciful toward people who did not even ask for his mercy. He noticed the sorrow of the widow of Nain (Lk. 7:1–17); he knew the pain of the Gerasene demoniac (Mk. 5:1–13); he could feel the frustrated hope of the man by the pool of Siloam (Jn. 5:2–9); he was touched by the infirmity of the woman who had not been able to straighten herself up for eighteen years (Lk. 13:10–13). Unasked, he freed these people—from death, from sin, from evil spirits, from disease—because they touched him. And to those who asked ("Son of David, have mercy on me . . ."; "Heal my daughter . . ."; "Make us clean . . ."; "That I might see . . .") he gently responded, "Of course I want to heal you—to make you whole—to forgive your sins—to give you life and peace and joy."

The examples are fewer, but the Gospels relate incidents in the life of Jesus where he experienced the blessing of this Beatitude. People were actually able to show mercy to him—by letting him touch their hearts and by letting power go forth from them for his benefit: the sinful woman who washed the feet of Jesus with her tears (Lk. 7:36), the apostles who left all to follow him and to be his friends (Jn. 6:66), Nicodemus who spoke up for him (Jn. 7:45–52), the good thief on the cross (Lk. 23:39–43). And of course, Jesus received the comfort of the Father who sent angels to minister to him after the temptations at the beginning of his public life and during the agony in Gethsemane before his glorification.

I sometimes wonder whether, in our modern world, it is not much more difficult to accept the blessing than to give the mercy. People seem more and more willing to feel the hurt of others. Even the exasperation that we feel over the enormity of a problem like world hunger, the frustration that we feel at the seeming "untouchableness" of violence within society, and the sadness we feel when we hear of the sufferings of so many—near to us or far away—are testimony to the fact that our hearts are compassionate, open to being touched by the lives of others. Yet many—especially those who find themselves in any form of ministry—refuse, in the name of humility or strength, to accept the blessing that is promised when one is merciful. Ministers (whatever their ministry) are all too often reluctant to be ministered unto. They spend their time lifting others' burdens (parenting children, caring for a spouse, teaching students, feeding the hungry, visiting shut-ins, helping the handicapped, providing hospitality, counseling, administering a parish, healing the sick, etc.), and they generally do not want their lives to be burdensome to others, to sap the energy of their neighbors.

The promise of Jesus is that those who do mercy will receive mercy. Our stance as Christians—as a people who take that promise to heart—must be one that says, "I am willing to leave my heart open to be touched by the lives of my sisters and brothers—even if power goes forth from me for their benefit. And I am willing to leave my heart open—humbly—to let my life touch theirs, even if I become empowered through their mercy to me." That is the blessing. Blessed are the merciful, for they shall obtain mercy.

BLESSED ARE THE PURE IN HEART . . .

One of the unique characteristics of Jesus as a religious leader is the fact that he saw his life and his ministry in terms of another person. His purpose was to be the enfleshed Word of the Father. His goal was to help people realize that they could call their God "Abba." He did not do things on his own account, or for his own glory. Even his closest friends could not deter him from his fidelity to his God. Jesus was singlehearted in his relationship to God. This is why the blessing promised to the pure in heart was a blessing he enjoyed personally.

The evangelists tell many stories about the singleheartedness of Jesus. He seemed eager to let people know his motivations and to have them share his enthusiastic love for the Father. From his youth, he had a sense that he must be "in his Father's house" (Lk. 2:49), that is, determined to acknowledge God as his Father, and willing to leave all to do the Father's will. When tempted by Satan, he remained pure in heart by refusing to be other than what God called him to be (Mt. 4:1–11). He knew when to stay with people and when to move on, and his decisions were based on his purpose in life (Lk. 4:42–44). When he called people to follow him, he demanded the same singleness of purpose: those who would come with him must realize that they will have nowhere to lay their head, that they must "leave the dead to bury their own dead," and that there is no turning back if one is to be fit for the kingdom of God (Lk. 9:57–62). Nothing less than total commitment would do. Nor were vested interests acceptable.

Jesus was uncompromising in his preaching and in the things he did. He claimed that his food was to do the will of the one who sent him (Jn. 4:34), and he challenged the death-dealing aspect of the law (Mt. 5–8; Mk. 3:16) and the hypocrisy of the scribes and Pharisees. He chased moneylenders out of his Father's house (Jn. 2:13–16) and ate in the homes and company of those who needed him—those for whom he had been sent (Mt. 9:10–13). He would not bow to false authority (Lk. 20:1–8; Jn. 19:10–11), nor would he consider compromising his mission—even to escape death at the hands of those who hated him (Mt. 16:21–23; Jn. 12:20–32).

The result of this purity of heart of Jesus was that he could see God. His relationship to his God was clear. He knew that the Father loved him and delighted in him (Mt. 3:13–17; Mk. 9:1–7), he knew that he was being transformed by the fidelity of his own life (Jn. 8:48–51), and he knew who the Father himself was and how the Father revealed himself (Mt. 11:25–30; Jn. 14:8–11).

If God does not seem to be very "visible" in our day, might this invisibility not be a function of our purity of heart? Or does the promise of the Beatitude apply only to the end of time? In ministry, for example, people are often motivated, in part, by a need to be helpful, to be of service, to be needed. This is really a positive motivating force and is possibly that place through which the Holy Spirit was able to inspire the person to minister to others. That need can be one that, like Jesus himself, directs us wholeheartedly to the Father. How often, though, in ministry do we become entangled in vested interests? When we compromise the word of God, when we water down the message of Jesus in order to maintain a degree of popularity or to build up our own little kingdoms, then we lose sight of our God and worship new idols. Those idols (power, influence, glory, "clout," a following, even money) affect who we are as Church and turn our zeal for the word of God into a debilitating fear of the power of evil. Then we find ourselves in a Church that resembles a bomb shelter. Its leaders overprotect their people and the Body closes in on itself. When we are caught up in this kind of idolatry, we become involved in survival rather than service, and our proclamation of the next world (where God is) prevents us from really seeing the suffering and the oppressed of this world (where God is).

Look at those in your life, for example, who are truly effective ministers. Or look at those who are truly great Church leaders. These are surely examples of people who have not had vested interests, who have not compromised the word of God, who have been singlehearted in their love for God and for his people. A good bet is that they see God. Blessed are the pure in heart, for they shall see God.

BLESSED ARE THE PEACEMAKERS ...

In addition to the Beatitude, Jesus refers to peace quite often in his preaching. It is obvious that peace is a value to him, as it was to the Jews of his day. The word "peace" (shalom) was a common Jewish greeting. Peace, in fact, was the long-awaited messianic gift. And so, when Jesus healed people or forgave their sins, he bade them: "Go in peace" (Mk. 5:34; Lk. 7:50; 8:48). When he sent the seventy-two on their mission, he told them to bless those who welcomed them, and to say: "Peace be to this house" (Lk. 10:3–12). When people confused messianic peace with neutrality or indecision about him, Jesus told them that they would have to take a stand, to make a choice: "Do you think that I have come to give peace on earth? No, I tell you, but rather division" (Lk. 12:51). All through his ministry, Jesus forgave others and encouraged everyone to be at peace: "Love your enemies" (Lk. 6:27).

It is, however, two passages from John's Gospel which tell us most about Jesus as peacemaker. For peacemakers act—and the call in this Beatitude is a call to be an active cause of peace in the world. In John 14, when Jesus is celebrating the passover with his friends, he promises the messianic gift of peace to them: he bids them not be troubled (14:1), he gives them hope in the power they will receive from him to do even greater works than they have seen him do (14:12), he reminds them once again of the great commandments to love God and each other (14:15–17), and he assures them that the Spirit, the Comforter, the Counselor, will help them know the truth (14:26). All of this is summed up finally in the promise: "Peace I leave with you; my peace I give you; not as the world gives do I give to you. Let not your hearts be troubled, neither let them be afraid" (14:27).

After the resurrection, Jesus once again speaks to his friends of peace. This time he tells them that he has kept his promise and that it is actually being fulfilled in them. The Jewish greeting, "Peace be with you," has taken on a new meaning. Jesus has become the Peacemaker through his death and resurrection. He has taken on to himself all of the burdens that we carry and that can take away real peace. He tells us that we are now free. And then he once again calls us to be active peacemakers in our world:

> Jesus said to them again, "Peace be with you. As the Father has sent me, even so I send you." And when he had said this, he breathed on them, and said to them, "Receive the Holy Spirit. If you forgive the sins of any, they are forgiven; if you retain the sins of any, they are retained." (Jn. 20:21–23)

It is this Spirit—breathed forth by Jesus—that is the blessing of this Beatitude. Jesus knew that he was the Son of God, and when he died, in that "one perfect sacrifice of peace," even those responsible for his death called him Son of God (Mt. 27:54). St. Paul would later write:

> For all who are led by the Spirit of God are sons of God. For you did not receive the spirit of slavery to fall back into fear, but you have received the spirit of sonship. When we cry, "Abba! Father!" it is the Spirit himself bearing witness with our spirit that we are children of God. (Rom. 8:15–17)

Our age will probably not go down in history as an age of great peace. We are warriors, armed to destroy the earth, and busy about the business of preserving peace by stockpiling still more weapons and by cleverly inventing newer, more sophisticated, more efficiently death-dealing "peace-makers." At the same time, the "feeling of peace" has become a holy stamp of approval for "whatever." In a caricatured form, or between the lines, some attitudes that are prevalent about "peace" would read like the following: "Sure, the government is using my tax money to develop the neutron bomb, but the situation is complex, and I'm at peace with continuing to pay my taxes." "Sure I realize that there are people who are dying of hunger in my city, but we're doing all we can to encourage the government to provide emergency food programs. I'm at peace with all of this." "Sure, somebody should continue to speak out against discrimination and against the anti-values of consumer society, but I'm at peace with the idea that the Church has a spiritual message to give and that we shouldn't get involved with these political issues."

The fact is that peace is not a feeling. It is a gift that comes from the Messiah, a gift that calls forth our participation in the peace-making activity of the Savior of the world. His promise of peace was kept through his dying for his friends. It would have nothing to do with the sword (Mt. 26:52–53). The peacemaking activity of Jesus, in a sense, was the living out of those values fostered by the previous six Beatitudes. It was an activity by which Jesus became a countersign, a life-giver, a lover par-excellence (Jn. 15:13). And we, his Church, must be that countersign in our world. It is only then that the world will recognize us as "his disciples." It is only then that we will be called children of God. Blessed are the peacemakers, for they shall be called children of God.

BLESSED ARE THOSE WHO ARE PERSECUTED FOR JUSTICE' SAKE . . .

If you are recognizable as a countersign to the established order, you have to expect that the established order will begin to be uncomfortable with your presence and activities. It was not long before those with vested interests in the status quo began persecuting Jesus. And how could it be otherwise? The man forgave sins—or claimed that he could (Blessed are the merciful . . .); he was sensitive to the needs of others and he dared to heal on the sabbath (Blessed are the meek . . .); he was so insolent as to denounce the evil practices and the hypocrisy of the scribes and Pharisees (Blessed are the pure in heart . . .); he defied the law by refusing to stone the woman caught in adultery (Blessed are the peacemakers . . .); he proclaimed publicly that human relationships were more important than the law (Blessed are those who hunger and thirst for justice . . .); he associated with—even identified with—those who are the least in the eyes of the "important" (Blessed are the poor in spirit . . .); and he had the audacity to complain to the "establishment" that they were piling up too many burdens on the people (Blessed are those who mourn . . .). And for all of this, Jesus must die! "The Pharisees went out, and immediately held counsel with the Herodians against him, how to destroy him" (Mk. 3:6).

Time and again, as Jesus realized what was in store for him, as he felt the hatred of the officials, and as he sparred with them in their attempts to trick him, he warned his disciples, "If the world hates you, know that it has hated me before it hated you. . . . If they persecuted me, they will persecute you" (Jn. 15:18–27). Still, the encouragement to his disciples was not to "run for cover," nor was it to establish a mode of being in the world that, at all costs, would offend no one. Rather, he spoke honestly and uncompromisingly:

> They will deliver you up to tribulation, and put you to death; and you will be hated by all nations for my name's sake. And then many will fall away, and betray one another, and hate one another. And many false prophets will arise and lead many astray. And because wickedness is multiplied, most men's love will grow cold. But he who endures to the end will be saved. And this gospel of the kingdom will be preached throughout the whole world, as a testimony to all nations; and then the end will come. (Mt. 23:9–14)

Jesus himself persevered to the end, and in the end he was vindicated. He stood before his disciples as the risen Lord and said to them, "All authority in heaven and on earth has been given to me" (Mt. 28:18). He knew he had been blessed with the kingdom.

Part of our problem in the Church today is that we don't seem to be doing much that is worthy of such persecution. We, more often than not, confirm, protect, defend, build up, support, buy into the status quo. We are consumerist, and racist, and sexist; we don't speak too loudly against the immorality of nuclear arms or mass starvation or discrimination or the anti-people use of technology or the mind-destroying process we call education. I'm not complaining here about the institutional Church. I'm referring to all too large a segment of the people of God. We are the ones who must hear the challenge in the words of Christ. We are the ones, individually and communally, who must be distinguishable as a people who live for justice and who are willing even to be persecuted and to die for the sake of justice. It is those who value this kind of integrity and live by it who are really part of the kingdom. Blessed are those who are persecuted for the sake of justice; the kingdom of God is theirs.

Jesus was a Beatitude person. The values he proclaimed were values that he lived by, and the blessings he promised were blessings that were part of his life. He knew that those blessings were the natural result of human beings striving to be ever more human.

BEATITUDE ATTITUDE	VALUES	BLESSING
Blessed are the poor in spirit	detachment, sharing of goods, freedom	theirs is the kingdom of heaven
Blessed are those who mourn	life, humanity	they shall be comforted
Blessed are the meek	gentleness, sensitivity, humility, non-violence	they shall inherit the earth
Blessed are those who hunger and thirst for justice	relationships	they shall be satisfied
Blessed are the merciful	mercy, forgiveness, compassion	they shall obtain mercy
Blessed are the pure in heart	singleheartedness, refusal to compromise the word of God	they shall see God
Blessed are the peacemakers	reconciliation, peace	they shall be called children of God
Blessed are those who are persecuted for justice' sake	integrity	theirs is the kingdom of heaven

What he called us to in that Sermon on the Mount was a life lived to the fullest, enjoyed because of its freedom, made perfect because of its honesty, connected to God's own life because of its care and concern for all others on this planet.

The call hearkens back to a call made by Yahweh long before to the people of Israel:

> I call heaven and earth to witness against you this day, that I have set before you life and death, blessing and curse; therefore choose life, that you and your descendants may live, loving the Lord your God, obeying his voice, and cleaving to him; for that means life to you and length of days, that you may dwell in the land which the Lord swore

to your fathers, to Abraham, to Isaac, and to Jacob, to give them (Dt. 30:19–20).

The call is ours still today. And our response lies in putting on the Lord Jesus, in taking his values as our own, and in letting the whole world know that our God is a God of the living—and one who blesses his people.

FAITH EXPERIENCE IV

Faith Experience IV helps us to take a closer look at the Beatitudes and to share our own experiences of having those values and of receiving the promised blessings. As with the other Faith Experiences, this format does not presuppose that the group involved in the faith sharing has been together before—nor even that the participants know each other. There is time for personal prayer during this Faith Experience, and even though the sharing is based primarily on Matthew 5:1–12, all should be encouraged to bring Bibles with them to these sessions. There are seven sessions altogether, including two eucharistic liturgies.

Session I

The first session begins in basically the same way as the first sessions of Faith Experiences II and III. This is a time for introductions (if necessary), for the Tuner to say a bit about the entire format and something about faith sharing itself, and for the group to agree on some basic ground rules to be followed during the faith sharing. The Tuner then leads the group into a prayer and sharing session to let the participants reflect on and share with each other how God has been active (or not) in their lives in the last few months. It is recommended that there be fifteen minutes of silence to begin this activity. Then the group could either (a) talk about their recent experience of God by choosing a Scripture passage that best exemplifies that experience, reading the passage, saying a few words about why it was chosen, and offering a short prayer, or (b) do simple faith sharing followed by an extended (say fifteen minutes) shared prayer. The difference between the two is that the first is basically a shared prayer session and the atmosphere maintained during that kind of sharing generally seems quieter and more prayerful. Both are good, simple ways of going about this initial session.

Sessions II and III

Session II will follow the same progression of activities as Session III. It is only the topic for sharing that will change in the two sessions. First, the Tuner begins the session by reading Matthew's version of the Beatitudes (5:1–12) and by saying a few words (a brief, meditative reflection) about what Jesus was saying in that Sermon on the Mount. The purpose of this reflection is to attune the participants to what will be the context for their faith sharing. Next, the people go off on their own for one hour of prayer and reflection on the question for sharing. And finally (after a coffee break, if desired) the group reassembles for one and a half to two hours of faith sharing.

In Session II, all are asked to consider the first part of each Beatitude—what we might refer to as the condition for the blessing, or the value to be lived, or the attitude to which we are called. Perhaps a chart such as the one just detailed in this chapter would be a helpful thing to reproduce and have available for each member of the group. The Tuner might also encourage the participants to reflect on these "conditions for Beatitude" from two different vantage points. It is possible to experience these conditions (a) because they have been forced on me or (b) because I have freely chosen them. Voluntary poverty, for example, is a different experience from the poverty imposed by society or life circumstance, giving mercy when asked is a different experience from initiating merciful activity, and hungering and thirsting for justice when one is oppressed is different from hungering and thirsting for justice when one is free.

The sharing is to be on the questions: How have I experienced these things in my life? When have I found myself especially called to live these values? (The Tuner might want to help the reflection and sharing by suggesting that each person pick at least three of the Beatitudes to talk about. This is so that all will know that there is no need to talk about all eight, nor is it desirable to focus on only one.) The session should close with a brief period of shared prayer.

In Session III, after a rereading of the Beatitudes and a few words from the Tuner, an hour is spent in personal prayer and reflection, this time on the second part of each Beatitude. The question for the sharing will be: How have I experienced these blessings in my life? This kind of sharing will probably naturally lead into a shared prayer of thanksgiving for those blessings.

Session IV

This session is a eucharistic celebration. At this point in the faith sharing, the participants have been looking at the *personal* impact of the Beatitudes. Now, in liturgy, the focus is shifted to the *societal* dimension of Christ's message. We suggest here one way of achieving this; there are certainly others. It is up to the Tuner to know the resources within the group and to plan this liturgical celebration accordingly.

Our suggestion is to have a simple liturgy based on the encyclical letter of Pope Paul VI "On the Development of Peoples" ("Populorum Progressio"). This letter articulates what the Christian stance should be in a world where "men are seeking to find a more secure food supply, cure for diseases, steady employment, increasing personal responsibility with security from oppression and freedom from degradation endangering the dignity of man, better education," and where, at the same time, "great numbers are living in conditions which frustrate their just desires" (n. 6). The excerpts below give some examples of how the values of the Beatitudes must be operative as we live the societal dimension of Christianity. Our relationship to our brothers and sisters around the world must reflect the fact that we *are* members of one human family and that we have responsibility for and to each other.

This liturgy could include the following elements:

(a) a penitential rite that is a communal acknowledgement of our sinfulness as a society;
(b) a reading of excerpts from the encyclical, along with the Gospel passage on the Beatitudes;
(c) a short reflection on the Church's social teaching;
(d) a rite of peace which focuses on the sign of peace as a sign of our willingness to be peacemakers on a global level.

THE BEATITUDES
AND EXCERPTS FROM "POPULORUM PROGRESSIO"

We present here the eight Beatitudes as they are reflected in Pope Paul VI's encylical. If this is used as part of the liturgy in Session IV, the ideal would be that the participants have had a chance to read the whole encyclical prior to the Faith Experience itself. A limited number of sections are referred to here; there are certainly many more examples, in this letter, of the proclamation of the Spirit of the Beatitudes.

BLESSED ARE THE POOR IN SPIRIT. "The acquisition of earthly possessions can lead man to inordinate desire, to seeking ever more plentiful resources, to the will to increase his own power. The avarice of individuals, of families, and of nations can affect the poorer no less than the richer, and can drive both to *materialism* which stifles their souls" (n. 18; see also n. 43).

BLESSED ARE THOSE WHO MOURN. "While so many people are going hungry, while so many families are suffering destitution, while so many people spend their lives submerged in the darkness of ignorance, while so many schools, hospitals, homes worthy of the name, are needed, every public or private squandering, every expenditure either of nations or individuals made for the sake of pretentious parade, finally every financially depleting arms race—all these, we say, become a scandalous and intolerable crime. The most serious obligation enjoined on us demands that we openly denounce it. Would that those in authority listened to us before it is too late" (n. 53; see also nn. 66 and 69).

BLESSED ARE THE MEEK. "Would that individuals, social groups and whole nations joined hands in a brotherly manner, and that the strong, setting aside their own advantage, would help the weak to make progress, devoting all their wisdom, enthusiasm, and charity to the task" (n. 75; see also nn. 65 and 82).

BLESSED ARE THOSE WHO HUNGER AND THIRST FOR JUSTICE. "The complete development of the individual must be joined with that of the human race and must be accomplished by mutual effort. In the city of Bombay we said: 'Man must meet man, nation meet nation as brothers and sisters, as children of God. With this mutual good will and friendship, with this sacred harmony of minds we must in like manner undertake the task of providing the future common prosperity of the human race'" (n. 43; see also nn. 3, 44, and 73).

BLESSED ARE THE MERCIFUL. "No one may look with indifference on the lot of his brothers who are still weighed down by such poverty and afflicted with ignorance and pining away with insecurity. The soul of every Christian must be moved by these miseries as Christ was when he said: 'I have compassion on the multitude'" (n. 74; see also n. 81).

BLESSED ARE THE PURE IN HEART. "It is not enough to combat destitution, urgent and necessary as this is. The point at issue is the establishment of a human society in which everyone, regardless of race, religion or nationality, can live a truly human life free from bondage imposed by men and the forces of nature not sufficiently mastered, a society in which freedom is not an empty word, and where Lazarus the poor man can sit at the same table as the rich man" (n. 47; see also n. 86).

BLESSED ARE THE PEACEMAKERS. "When we combat misery and struggle against injustice, we are providing not only for man's prosperity but also for his spiritual and moral development and are therefore promoting the welfare of the whole human race. Indeed peace is not simply to be reduced to the elimination of all war, as if it consisted in a precarious balance of power. Peace is achieved by constant effort day after day" (n. 76; see also nn. 31, 45, 51, 63 and 75).

BLESSED ARE THOSE PERSECUTED FOR JUSTICE' **SAKE.** "This striving for a more human way of life does indeed demand effort and entails inconveniences but these very sufferings endured out of love for our brothers and for their benefit can be most conducive to the development of the human race" (n. 79; see also n. 80).

Session V

More often than not, the things we believe and the values we espouse in our own lives have come to us through people who have lived those beliefs and values before us and who have become our models or heroes/heroines. Session V provides an enjoyable, relaxing way of sharing those persons with others. It is a story-telling session during which all are asked to tell about one or two people who have especially lived out the values of the Beatitudes. The Tuner should set an informal tone to this session, encourage people to be relaxed and to simply give anecdotes about their "Beatitude people." In a sense what the anecdotes should bring out is something like, "I wish you had known this person (or been there when this person . . .) because then you would have seen the real meaning of this Beatitude."

It is recommended that the Tuner explain this session at the end of Session III (if the group is doing this Faith Experience in a weekend format) so that the participants can have time to think about the people they want to share with the group. When Session V begins, the Tuner determines a pattern for the sharing (for example, each person gets a chance to tell one story before "seconds" are allowed), and reads a passage from Scripture (Lk. 7:24–30 and 10:29–37 are good story-telling passages). After a few moments of silence, the story-telling begins. Shared prayer brings this session to a close.

Session VI

After the long periods of reflection and sharing in the previous sessions, the group now focuses on the present and the future, as well as on the *communal* aspect of living the Beatitudes. The sharing for this session is based on two questions: What do I need most in order to be a "Beatitude person"? What do we (this Christian community, this parish, this Church) need most to be a "Beatitude people"? This is not intended to be a negative type of sharing, where complaints are lodged against self and community. Rather, it is to be a time of reflection on the deepest desires we have for our personal growth and for the growth of the community to which we belong.

As usual, the Tuner is responsible for setting the desired tone for this type of sharing. A reading from Scripture (Mt. 6:25–34, Mk. 8:1–10, and Lk. 19:1–10 are good passages here) and fifteen minutes of silent prayer and reflection should precede the sharing.

Session VII

The final session of Faith Experience IV includes faith sharing in the form of a response to the others in the group, and a closing liturgy. The sharing can be done as part of the liturgy of the word, or the liturgy can be celebrated as a closing prayer for the session (as well as for the entire Faith Experience). The exercise is similar to the Christ seal of Faith Experience I, but the focus is different.

Since the group has been looking at the personal, communal and societal dimensions of the Beatitudes, the response aims at an integration of the three levels. Each participant is asked to reflect to the others in the group: How do I see values of the Beatitudes in your life, and how do I see that you use these values (or could use them) for the building up of the people of God: This exercise can be done in the same way that the Christ seal was done.

An interesting alternative is to arrange to have available a sheet of paper for each of the members of the group (sometime between Session V and this one) to write down reflections about the person in the form of a new Beatitude. In other words, the participants say to each other, "Blessed are you, because. . . ." If this is done, Session VII is one during which each one reads the Beatitudes that have been written about him/her by the other members of the community, and responds (in some form of ordered sharing) to what others have written.

It is the spirit with which Jesus lived his life that is reflected in the Beatitudes. We, too, seek to live by that spirit and to help each other to become Beatitude people. It is this desire that must remain at the basis of the sharing that is done in this Faith Experience.

The following is a synopsis of Faith Experience IV (The Beatitudes) as it fits into a weekend schedule.

SESSION I

Friday Evening—7:30–9:00

(a) The Tuner invites the participants to introduce themselves to one another (if necessary), gives a short introduction to faith sharing, and sets down some basic guidelines for the weekend.

(b) The Tuner then sets the tone for the first exercise.

(c) Prayer from Scripture: (1) Fifteen minutes of personal prayer and reflection; each chooses a passage from Scripture which expresses his/her present relationship with God. (2) Sharing: reading of passage and brief explanation of why it was chosen. (3) Close with a communal prayer of praise or a song.

SESSION II

Saturday Morning—9:00–12:00

(a) The Tuner reads the Beatitudes (Matthew 5:1–12) and leads the group in a brief, meditative reflection on this passage.

(b) The Tuner should then give a brief overview of the day.

(c) The participants spend one hour in personal prayer and reflection on the first part of each Beatitude, that is, the condition for the blessing. The questions for the sharing will be: How have I experienced these things (poverty, being merciful, etc.) in my life? When have I found myself especially called to live these values?

(d) Faith sharing on the above questions.

(e) A brief period of shared prayer.

SESSION III

Saturday Afternoon—1:30–4:30

(a) The Tuner sets the tone for this session by rereading Matthew 5:1–12.

(b) One hour of personal prayer—this time focusing on the second part of each Beatitude, that is, the blessings. The question for the sharing will be: How have I experienced these blessings in my life?

(c) Faith sharing on the above question.

(d) A brief period of shared prayer.

SESSION IV

Saturday Afternoon—5:00–6:00

This session is a eucharistic liturgy which highlights the societal dimensions of Christ's message in the Beatitudes. Some of the liturgy of the word could be a consideration of Pope Paul VI's encyclical, "On the Development of Peoples." This chapter contains some references to that letter.

SESSION V

Saturday Evening—7:30–9:30

(a) The Tuner sets the tone for this session by reading a passage from Scripture (e.g., Lk. 7:24–30 or 10:29–37) and explains the activity that the group will be involved in. (It might be good for the Tuner to offer an explanation of this session at the end of Session III in order to give the participants some time to prepare.)

(b) Story-telling about "Beatitude people" in our lives; this is a time for talking about people who have taught us the real meaning of the Beatitudes by living them out themselves.

(c) A brief period of shared prayer, especially in thanksgiving for the people spoken of in the stories.

SESSION VI

Sunday Morning—9:00–10:00

(a) The Tuner sets the tone for this session by reading a passage from Scripture (e.g., Mt. 6:25–34; Mk. 8:1–10; Lk. 19:1–
10), and explains the sharing that will take place.

(b) Faith sharing based on two questions: What do I need most
in order to be a "Beatitude person"? What do we (this Christian community, this parish, this Church) need most in order to be a "Beatitude people"?

SESSION VII

Sunday Morning—10:30–12:00

(a) Faith sharing on: How do we see new Beatitudes in the people around us? This can be done in the same way that the
Christ seal was done in Faith Experience I; an alternative
way is explained in this chapter.

(b) A closing eucharistic liturgy.

5

Faith Experience V

FAITH AND JUSTICE

> _Jesus then said to the Jews who had believed in him,
> "If you continue in my word, you are truly my dis-
> ciples, and you will know the truth, and the truth
> will make you free." They answered him, "We are de-
> scendants of Abraham, and have never been in bond-
> age to anyone. How is it that you say, 'You will be
> free'?" Jesus answered them, "Truly, truly, I say to
> you, everyone who commits sin is a slave to sin. The
> slave does not continue in the house forever; the son
> continues forever. So if the son makes you free, you
> will be free indeed."_
>
> _Jn. 8:31–36_

The popular Church seems to be moving—ever so slowly and cautiously—into a new age, characterized by the communal "ownership" of doctrine that has been very eloquently set forth by the institutional Church for quite a long time. At least, many of God's people are now struggling with the very difficult question of the Church's (and of their own personal) role in the quest for justice in our world. From Leo XIII to John Paul II, our leaders have taught that justice for all people is a special concern of the Church and that work for justice is part of the Church's mission. Since Pope John XXIII and the Second Vatican Council, the Church's stance toward the question of justice has been a call to the whole world. We members of the Church must continue reflecting on that social teaching and on its implications for us as believers. The pages that follow are a reflection on Jesus as one who proclaimed justice, on the Church's social teaching, and on what an adult Christian stance in the world might be in light of what we believe about Jesus and his Church.

103

JESUS CHRIST, LIBERATOR

It is not at all unusual for Christians to look upon Jesus as the liberator of humanity. We have all learned about our slavery to sin and about the new passover through which Jesus, the new Moses, delivered us from that slavery to the new freedom of the children of God. The promised land of the New Testament, the land of freedom, is that place where Jesus dwells within us as one who died for the forgiveness of sins and as one who makes good for us that promise of freedom. Jesus was a reconciler, and through reconciliation he liberated.

We have learned, too, that Jesus performed miracles that freed people from all sorts of disease—from paralysis and leprosy, from demonic possession and even from death. He also performed miracles that freed people from the forces of nature (for example, the storm at sea—Mk. 4:35–41) and that freed people to use nature more effectively (for example, the multiplication of the loaves and fishes—Mt. 15:32–39). Jesus was a healer, and through his miracles of healing he liberated.

Having learned all of this, however, our experience of Church and of believers in Jesus Christ is by and large not one of a group that rejoices in freedom. There is generally a cautious, somber timidity in the air when the conversation turns—as it all too rarely does—to the tremendous implications of having a God who died to give us freedom. It is as though Jesus overcame death, but death could make a comeback; as though Jesus poured out his blood for the forgiveness of sin, but sin could still "win out" in the end; as though we had been freed by Jesus, but we had better not enjoy that freedom lest, in the very enjoying of it, we lose it again.

The saving actions of Jesus speak to us certain truths about him, and about us. Our beliefs, because of Jesus, are that humanity had to be redeemed, that Jesus calls all of us to be with him in the mystery of his passion, death, and resurrection, and that he brought spiritual freedom to his people. These benefits, surely, are not unusual. But the conclusions we would draw from them are not what we learned early in life, nor do they correspond to what we often hear from fellow Christians.

In many people, there seems to be a nagging little voice that jumbles the truth about Jesus and about Christianity, and that keeps them from coming to a full realization of what Jesus really did and said when he walked this earth. These would conclude that if humanity had to be redeemed, then it must be evil, and that if

Jesus calls us to be with him in his paschal mystery, then we must be destined to suffer and we should even seek out suffering in this life, and that if the freedom that Jesus brought was spiritual, then it must not be confused with human freedom that is so often selfishly sought by so many.

I believe that what Jesus said in redeeming humanity is that it is *good* and worth redeeming. I believe that Jesus tried to wipe out suffering and death, and that his invitation is one to unite whatever suffering comes to us naturally to his own suffering, death *and resurrection* so that no amount of pain or dying will be able to leave us without the hope of living again. I believe that what Jesus said about humanity most strongly—especially through his own humanity— was that it *is* spiritual, and that spiritual freedom is really, in truth, human freedom in all its dimensions.

Part of the problem is that we do not go far enough in listening to what Jesus proclaimed as *truth* for us to live by. Belief in Jesus should bring us to an awareness of this man as a liberator of the whole person. The truth that Jesus proclaimed had to do with how persons relate to persons, and how our willingness to acknowledge others and to treat them with the dignity that is their due leads to righteousness—to justice—and, consequently, to true freedom. "If you continue in my word, you are truly my disciples, and you will know the truth, and the truth will make you free" (Jn. 8:31–32).

One need only read the words of Jesus to hear in them his strong plea (his command) that we *do justice* in every area of life. One need only attend carefully to the life of Jesus to see that what he tried to do all along was to point out the truth of our relationship with God, of our relationship to each other, of our relationship to the world. If justice means attending to relationships and bringing order to those relationships (and justice essentially means just that), then the Gospel is a Gospel of justice and Jesus as liberator meant us to be free, not only from sin and death, but also from oppression and poverty and hunger and alienation and all shackles made by human hands.

Jesus Christ, the liberator, told us that God was *not* a monster or a harsh taskmaster, but a loving Father. He introduced us again to a loving, gentle God who only wants life for us and who calls us to care for each other as members of a loving family would care for each other (see Lk. 15:11–32; 11:1–13).

Jesus Christ, the liberator, told us that the harshness of the Mosaic law was to be replaced by the new law of love which we could find personified in him:

- "Love one another as I have loved you" (Jn. 15:12).
- "Has no one condemned you? . . . Neither do I condemn you; go and do not sin again" (Jn. 8:10–11).
- And Jesus said to him, "What do you want me to do for you?" And the blind man said to him, "Master, let me receive my sight." And Jesus said to him, "Go your way; your faith has made you well" (Mk. 10:51–52).
- "I am unwilling to send them away hungry, lest they faint on the way" (Mt. 15:32).
- "They need not go away; you give them something to eat" (Mt. 14:16).
- "He who is greatest among you shall be your servant" (Mt. 23:11).
- "I was hungry and you gave me food, I was thirsty and you gave me drink, I was a stranger and you welcomed me, I was naked and you clothed me, I was sick and you visited me, I was in prison and you came to me. . . . As you did it to one of the least of these my brethren, you did it to me" (Mt. 25:35–40).
- "I do not pray for these only, but also for those who believe in me through their word, that they may all be one" (Jn. 17:20).

Jesus Christ, the liberator, told us that the world was gift, not enemy, and that the gift must be cherished and cared for, and that it could give us life. He used nature, and its perfect ordering, to teach us about life and its possibilities. And he invited us to be in such a relationship with the world that it would continue teaching us (see Mt. 16:1–3).

Is our faith in this kind of liberator one that could lead us to believe in freedom from political oppression as a spiritual value? Can we believe that freedom from hunger is part of the spiritual freedom proclaimed by Jesus Christ? Are just wages, and human rights, and the dignity of all peoples part of the spiritual message of our Savior? Will we—can we ever—be truly free if we only seek out sacramental absolution from our sins, but do not pay attention to the thousands of political prisoners, the ugly racism, the unjust working conditions, the starvation, the silencing, the violence that infect our political world with diseases that are fatal for so many?

Is our faith the kind that dulls our appreciation of how people suffer? Is it a faith that leads us to shrug our shoulders in helpless acceptance of the fact that "there will always be evil in our world, and some must, unfortunately, suffer—but God must want it that way"?

It was *humanity—human persons*—that Jesus liberated. And wherever humanity is shackled—unfree—the work of Jesus is frustrated. If someone dies of hunger, if violence keeps a neighborhood in constant fear, if a worker does not get a salary sufficient to support his or her family, if technology is used to destroy life, if a group of people denies the dignity of another group, if a dictator oppresses an entire country, if a legislature passes a bad law, if a system keeps poor people poor while allowing the rich to get richer, if a structure of society denies basic human rights to people—is not all of this doing violence to our belief in what Jesus lived and died for?

All of those situations—human, political, worldly situations—are occasions through which the human spirit is constantly being broken on our planet. They are situations with spiritual implications. And our faith in Jesus Christ must carry us to that point where we will be willing to choose freedom for ourselves and for our world. We must let our faith in the liberator of humanity carry us to a point where we will refuse to tolerate injustice at any level and where we will give up whatever must be given up to bring to light the truth about how we stand in relationship to each other. Living in the spirit of Jesus, we will come to know that truth, and the truth will make us free.

THE CHURCH'S SOCIAL TEACHING

To do justice to the social teaching of the Church would probably require a reprinting of all major writings of Popes, bishops, and bishops' conferences that have addressed the issue of justice. The documents are mostly brilliant, sensitive, human, spiritual reflections on the world, on the sufferings of humanity, and on the rights and responsibilities of each individual, of every nation and of the Church toward all people and toward all of creation. In May 1978 the National Conference of Catholic Bishops of the United States published a document entitled, "To Do the Work of Justice—A Plan of Action for the Catholic Community in the United States." This is a follow-up document to the "Bicentennial Call to Action," and in it the American Bishops wrote: "In Catholic thought, social justice is not merely a secular or humanitarian matter. Social justice is a reflection of God's respect and concern for each person and an effort to protect the essential human freedom necessary for each person to achieve his or her destiny as a child of God" (p. 5).

If there is anything sad or tragic about the life of Jesus, it is that so few people heard what he was saying. The speaking in parables was supposed to help people understand more clearly what Jesus was saying, but they remained confused (see Lk. 8:4–18). The directness of Jesus' words could have made his message unmistakable, but people only turned away from what they considered hard sayings (see Jn. 6:35–68). There is, likewise, something a bit sad and tragic about the social teaching of the Church. Basically, it is that this teaching is read or heard by so few of the Church's members.

It would be relevant here to quote a number of paragraphs from recent encyclicals and other Church documents on social justice for two reasons: first, to highlight what seem to be basic principles of Catholic social doctrine, and, second, to give a short, simple, direct indication of how well the Church actually does remain faithful to the word and spirit of Jesus in its proclamation of a Gospel of justice. (If you have not read these documents, a very good presentation of the Church's social teaching can be found in: *The Gospel of Peace and Justice—Catholic Social Teaching since Pope John,* by Joseph Gremillion, Orbis Books, 1976.)

Pope John XXIII was quite clear, in *Mater et Magistra,* that the demands of social justice were rooted in the need for the ordering of human relationships. He wrote:

What the Catholic Church teaches and declares regarding the social life and relationships of men is beyond question for all time valid. The cardinal point of this teaching is that individual men are necessarily the foundation, cause, and end of all social institutions. We are referring to human beings, insofar as they are social by nature, and raised to an order of existence that transcends and subdues nature. Beginning with this very basic principle whereby the dignity of the human person is affirmed and defended, Holy Church—especially during the last century and with the assistance of learned priests and laymen, specialists in the field—has arrived at clear social teachings whereby the mutual relationships of men are ordered. Taking general norms into account, these principles are in accord with the nature of things and the changed conditions of man's social life, or with the special genius of our day.

Moreover, these norms can be approved by all. . . . But today, more than ever, principles of this kind must not only be known and understood, but also applied to those systems and methods which the various situations of time and place either suggest or require. This is indeed a difficult, though lofty, task. Toward its fulfillment we exhort not only our brothers and sons everywhere, but all men of good will (MM 218–221).

Later on, in *Pacem in Terris,* he wrote of the responsibilities that political communities have toward each other:

Relations between political communities are, in addition, to be regulated by justice. This implies, over and above recognition of their mutual rights, the fulfillment of their respective duties. (PT 91)

In that same encyclical letter, the Pope urged all of the faithful— his children—to bring an explicit Christian dimension to the institutions and structures of society:

They should endeavor, therefore, in the light of their Christian faith and led by love, to insure that the various institutions—whether economic, social, cultural or political in purpose—should be such as not to create obstacles, but rather to facilitate or render less arduous man's perfecting of himself in both the natural order and the supernatural. (PT 146).

At the beginning of the Second Vatican Council, the Council Fathers acknowledged two urgent issues facing them and the whole Church: peace, and social justice. In their opening "Message to Humanity" they wrote:

The teaching expounded in (Pope John's) encyclical *Mater et Magistra* clearly shows that the Church is supremely necessary for the modern world if injustices and unworthy inequalities are to be denounced, and if the true order of affairs and of values is to be restored, so that man's life can become more human according to the standards of the Gospel. (MH 5)

In the Pastoral Constitution on the Church in the Modern World, *Gaudium et Spes,* the Council Fathers very strongly linked human aspirations with what is deepest in the hearts of the followers of Christ:

> Indeed, nothing genuinely human fails to raise an echo in their hearts. For theirs is a community composed of men. United in Christ, they are led by the Holy Spirit in their journey to the kingdom of their Father and they have welcomed the news of salvation which is meant for every man. That is why this community realizes that it is truly and intimately linked with mankind and its history (GS 1).

Pope Paul VI, the Pope of peace, continued the development of the Church's social doctrine in a great many documents. His "call to action" in the letter written to commemorate the eightieth anniversary of Leo XIII's encyclical (*Rerum Novarum*) brings into sharp focus the tremendous responsibility that we all have, individually and communally, to participate in the task of bringing about justice on our planet:

> It is to all Christians that we address a fresh and insistent call to action. In our encyclical On the Development of Peoples we urged that all should set themselves to the task: "Laymen should take up as their own proper task the renewal of the temporal order. If the role of the hierarchy is to teach and to interpret authentically the norms of morality to be followed in this matter, it belongs to the laity, without waiting passively for orders and directives, to take the initiative freely and to infuse a Christian spirit into the mentality, customs, laws and structures of the community in which they live." Let each one examine himself, to see what he has done up to now and what he ought to do. It is not enough to recall principles, state intentions, point to crying injustices and utter prophetic denunciations; these words will lack real weight unless they are accompanied for each individual by a livelier awareness of personal responsibility and by effective action. (OA 48)

Six months later, the 1971 Synod of Bishops produced a document entitled "Justice in the World," in which they strongly affirmed the place of the quest for justice in the work and mission of the Church:

> Listening to the cry of those who suffer violence and are oppressed by unjust systems and structures, and hearing the appeal of a world that by its perversity contradicts the plan of its Creator, we have shared our awareness of the Church's vocation to be present in the heart of the world. . . . The uncertainty of history and the painful convergences in the ascending path of the human community direct us to sacred history; there God has revealed himself to us, and made known to us, as it is brought progressively to realization, his plan of liberation and salvation which is once and for all fulfilled in the paschal mystery of Christ. Action on behalf of justice and participation in the transformation of the world fully appear to us as a constitutive dimension of the preaching of the Gospel, or, in other words, of the Church's mission for the redemption of the human race and its liberation from every oppressive situation. (JW 6)

Finally, in his first encyclical letter, *Redemptor Hominis,* Pope John Paul II asserted that the Church will continue in its plea and its work for justice:

> The Church, however, which has no weapons at its disposal apart from those of the spirit, of the word and of love, cannot renounce its proclamation of "the word . . . in season and out of season." For this reason it does not cease to implore each side of the two and to beg everybody in the name of God and in the name of man: Do not kill! Do not prepare destruction and extermination for men! Think of your brothers and sisters who are suffering from hunger and misery! Respect each one's dignity and freedom! (RH 58)

There is more, much more, that could be quoted, or highlighted, about the social teaching of the Church. The Church has addressed the questions of human rights, politics, disarmament, political refugees, unemployment, education, population, minorities, sexism, labor, family, economics, technology, religious freedom, international cooperation, hunger, culture, racism, and many, many more. "Indeed, nothing genuinely human fails to raise an echo" in the hearts of the followers of Christ.

What is important for us, at this point, is the fact that, insofar as the Church proclaims the same truth that Jesus proclaimed—the truth about how we must be in loving relationship to all of creation, in all its dimensions—it participates in the same activity of liberation that Jesus was involved in. And so we have in the Church truly a reflection of the Spirit of Jesus.

The problem that remains is that we, who are supposed to be animated by that Spirit, are often reluctant to take to heart this proclamation and teaching of the Church. The problem that remains is that our faith in Jesus Christ and our faith in his Church still do not lead us to a radical acceptance of our call to work for justice and freedom in our world.

At the very least, if we are to be faithful to Jesus Christ and to his Church, we must move in our questioning from whether the Church has any business being involved in this social justice "thing" to: "How can I, and we, as Church, work more effectively to promote justice in the world?" For the truth is that faith in Jesus and faith in his message must necessarily issue in the active promotion of justice among all people.

AN ADULT CHRISTIAN STANCE IN THE WORLD

It is a frightening and confusing prospect—this idea that faith issues in justice. Does this mean, for example, that if I do nothing about the international situations that violate human rights I am being unfaithful to my commitment to Jesus Christ? Does it mean that if I am not active in the fight against racism in my own country I am not a good Christian? Do I have to be "involved in politics" to be a follower of Jesus?

In issuing his "call to action," Pope Paul VI addressed these questions. He wrote: "Amid the diversity of situations, functions and organizations, each one must determine, in his conscience, the actions which he is called to share in" (OA 49). Later on, he asserts that "the same Christian faith can lead to different commitments" (OA 50). What remains indisputable is that the Holy Father issued the call to action "to all Christians" and asked "each one (to) examine himself, to see what he has done up to now, and what he ought to do" (OA 48).

In fact, the entire body of Catholic social teaching is a call to all of us to take an adult Christian stance in our world. That stance could be called one of "convert-able humanity": letting that humanity stand open to the kind of conversion that would turn all of creation toward Life itself and receive the fullness of that life. Our faith, our Savior, our Church, and our world, suffering and rejoicing, broken and healed—all seem to be calling forth from us that which is best in us: our humanity in all its glory, with all its potential.

We Christians must project justice in everything we do. Our faith must be one that, of necessity, celebrates humanity as the place where divinity dwells. It must be a faith that is intolerant of the destruction of human life, of the denigration of human dignity, of the breaking of the human spirit. Our faith must lead us to openly oppose injustice, oppression, and discrimination of any kind. Our faith must be the kind that moves the world from violence to gentleness, from selfishness and greed to generosity and sharing, from hatred to love, from sin to holiness.

For us to live that faith with integrity, we Christians must be willing to acknowledge our need for conversion, and we must take the steps necessary for that conversion to take place in us. Pope John XXIII insisted that the Church was always in need of reform. In saying this, he was setting an example for the contemporary Christian. It was a clear statement—not of ugliness or evil, but of a simple need to keep turning toward God, to change as the Spirit prompts, to move always in the direction of Jesus Christ.

Can anyone tell us that we must be involved in this or that as a measure of our fidelity to Jesus Christ? Must we boycott this product or is it necessary to sign that petition? Do we have to join this group or support that politician? Possibly these are the wrong questions to ask. To be an adult Christian in today's world means to be recognizable as a Christian; it means not hiding the fact that we are Christians; it means, in effect, becoming public figures because we openly, publicly profess the Lordship of Jesus, the liberator of the world, and fearlessly stand for what he stood for. Adult Christians stand in the world as public figures who know that they are sinners, redeemed by the blood of Jesus, convert-able to ever deeper humanity. They are public figures who know that the credibility of their faith will lie—for the non-believer—in their willingness to be just like their Lord who gave up his life out of love for them. They are public figures who sense keenly—and even identify with—the suffering and poverty and oppression of their brothers and sisters. Adult Christians stand in the world as public figures who are convinced that justice and freedom are the destiny, the right, the privilege of all humanity, and convinced, too, that justice will be done in the world the more they are willing to be converted personally and to proclaim "on rooftops" the amazing, joyful message of Jesus, the liberator of humanity.

In 1968, the second General Conference of Latin American Bishops took place in Medellín, Colombia. At this historic meeting, the bishops made this connection between our Christian faith and action for justice:

> The very God who creates . . . is the same God who, in the fullness of time, sends his Son in the flesh, so that he might come to liberate all men from the slavery to which sin has subjected them: hunger, misery, oppression, and ignorance—in a word, that injustice and hatred which have their origin in human selfishness. Thus, for our authentic liberation, all of us need a profound conversion so that "the kingdom of justice, love and peace" may come to us. The origin of all disdain for mankind, of all injustice, should be sought in the internal imbalance of human liberty, which will always need to be rectified in history. The uniqueness of the Christian message does not so much consist in the affirmation of the necessity for structural change, as it does in the insistence on the conversion of men which will in turn bring about this change. We will not have a new continent without new and reformed structures, but, above all, there will be no new continent without new men who know how to be truly free and responsible according to the light of the Gospel. (Medellín 3)

What, then, are the right questions? What should Christians be asking themselves? At least, we Christians should be asking what our personal call is with respect to "action on behalf of justice and participation in the transformation of the world" (JW 6). Are we *doing justice* where we live? Where do we need conversion? Have we developed a tolerance for injustice? Are we willing to isolate ourselves from the inhumanity of oppressive structures? Have we convinced ourselves that the problem is just too big and there is nothing that we can do? Are we content not to care about people who are too far away from us to touch us? Have we become willing to forget the existence of the hungry or of the politically oppressed in other parts of the world? Can we continue living with and caring for "our own"—and not acknowledge that we are part of a human family, a world community, and that all people are "our own"? Are there members of our family that we are willing to let die?

These are hard questions. Obviously no one can do everything. We must make choices. That's not the problem. The problem—the real threat to integral, faithful Christianity—is that we will be lulled into a "faith-stance" that neglects the "human" because ours is a "spiritual" message; a "faith-stance" that has no societal dimension, that does not challenge us to care for all people; a "faith-stance" that will ultimately bring to us that judgment promised by the One we have claimed all along to be following:

> "Depart from me, you cursed, into the eternal fire prepared for the devil and his angels; for I was hungry and you gave me no food, I was thirsty and you gave me no drink, I was a stranger and you did not welcome me, naked and you did not clothe me, sick and in prison and you did not visit me. . . . Truly, I say to you, as you did it not to one of the least of these, you did it not to me." (Mt. 25:41–46)

The closing paragraph of the NCCB document, *To Do the Work of Justice*, gives simple testimony to the Church as a people willing to live the full implications of faith in Jesus, the liberator. May we be such a people:

> We do not forget the fact that hundreds of people came to us to describe how their lives are troubled by social injustice. Others came to describe situations of injustice which they had seen or worked in. All came with hope that the Church can be a sign and source of social justice and peace in the world today. We have been moved by these voices. Perhaps the major result of this extensive consultation is the hope it has given us that together we can bear witness to the unity of the Church of Christ by the justice and peace in which we all live. (TD 30)

FAITH EXPERIENCE V

Faith Experience V is a sharing of our beliefs and experiences around the question of justice. In a sense, it is the most difficult of the Faith Experiences (along with FE VI which deals with the question of lifestyle) because its subject is one which is deeply puzzling—even problematic—for most people. This faith sharing format is structured around basic human experiences of justice and injustice, of our sense of order in our relationship to nature, technology and the human family, and our need for conversion. All of this is done within the context of faith in Jesus Christ, and includes one session where the group explicitly seeks out the connection between justice and Christian faith. There are seven sessions in this Faith Experience, including two eucharistic liturgies.

Session I

The first session begins with the usual introductions and explanations from the Tuner about faith sharing, the ground rules to be agreed upon, and the subject and orientation of this particular Faith Experience. After this, there should be a short "go-around" to allow all present to say briefly how they feel as they begin the Faith Experience, and what their expectations are for this time of faith sharing in which they will be engaged.

The Tuner then sets the tone for the beginning of sharing on faith and justice. This is best done by reading a short passage from Scripture, explaining the questions for sharing, and inviting the participants to spend fifteen minutes in silent prayer and reflection in order to "get in touch" with the Lord in their lives and to pull together their thoughts for the faith sharing.

For this session, the Tuner should read a passage that has something to do with human dignity (for example, Mt. 6:25–33; Ps. 8; Lk. 10:17–24), or with the need to do justice (see many of the sections of the Sermon on the Mount from Mt. 5–7 or Lk. 6:20–49). The participants are then asked to reflect on three experiences in their lives that they would share with the group: one having to do with coming to an awareness of their own dignity as a human being, another that recalls a personal experience (as agent or victim) of an injustice, and a third that is an experience (again either as agent or beneficiary) of an act of justice. In other words, all should ask themselves: How have I come to experience my own dignity as a human being? How have I experienced injustice in my life? How have I experienced justice in my life? These questions, and this initial sharing, are meant to help people to reflect, simply and briefly, on the fact that the considerations of human dignity and of justice and injustice touch our lives perhaps more often than we realize, and in ways we often do not even suspect.

Participants should be encouraged to focus on one example of each and to try to take three minutes or so for each experience. (This means that the sharing in this session would not extend beyond, say, an hour and a half for a group of eight or nine people.) The session should end with a brief period of shared prayer.

(Sessions II, III, and IV)

The next three sessions will follow the same basic format: a reading of Scripture, an explanation of the session by the Tuner, fifteen minutes of silent prayer and reflection, a sharing of experiences, and a short period of shared prayer. These sessions are meant to focus the participants on different aspects of our world and the lives we live in relationship to that world. Session V will then be one that pulls together all of these life experiences into the faith context.

Session II

The first area of life experience that will be the topic for sharing is *nature*. Our experience of nature, of the alive world around us, with its sunrises and sunsets, its oceans and mountains, its inner-city gardens, its birds and trees and cricket sounds, its snowfalls and wind storms—somehow all of these things have a power to speak to us of God. A friend once suggested to me that this was true because there is no injustice in the world of nature. It is well ordered. Its relationships are as they should be. And with this justice naturally comes an eloquence about the source of all creation.

This session is meant to be a simple sharing of our experiences of nature as this marvelous teacher about God. All are asked to recount two or three experiences of nature that became for them real experiences of God: faith experiences. The Tuner, in the explanation of this session, should say a few words to help the group to focus on the goal of this sharing and on the order that is to be found in nature, so that their choices of anecdotes will reflect something about the connection between faith and justice.

There are many good passages in the Bible that speak of the beauty of nature and that can be used at the beginning of this session to set the tone for the reflection and sharing. The creation account from the Book of Genesis, Psalm 104, and the "lilies of the field" passage from Matthew 6:25–33 are obvious and good examples.

Once again (and this would hold for all the sessions of the Faith

Experience) the Tuner should encourage a length of sharing for each person that will give all the opportunity to say something, if they want, in the time that is available. Obviously, the group could decide to extend the sharing time and let all the participants speak as long as they wish. One hour and a half is recommended as a good length for this session, as well as for the next one.

Session III

After looking at nature, the handiwork of God, the group now focuses on the work of human hands: *technology* in our world. It is a tremendous and awesome thing to consider how human beings have been able to use their ingenuity and creativity in fashioning all kinds of "creations" for the benefit of humanity. For example, the worlds of medicine and aviation and communications give brilliant testimony to the fact that new kinds of order brought to created things can result in new kinds of beauty in our world. Technology, if we let it, can also speak to us of God. The Second Vatican Council spoke of the work of human hands in this way:

> Thus, far from thinking that works produced by man's own talent and energy are in opposition to God's power, and that the rational creature exists as a kind of rival to the Creator, Christians are convinced that the triumphs of the human race are a sign of God's greatness and the flowering of his own mysterious design. For the greater man's power becomes, the farther his individual and community responsibility extends. Hence it is clear that men are not deterred by the Christian message from building up the world, or impelled to neglect the welfare of their fellows. They are, rather, more stringently bound to do these very things. (GS 34)

Session III begins with a reading from Scripture that will set the tone for the sharing. Psalm 8, Ecclesiasticus 17:3–10, Isaiah 32:1–8, and Isaiah 2:1–11 are good passages here. Then the participants are asked to spend fifteen minutes in silent prayer and reflection. The questions for the sharing are: How have I experienced technology as a force for justice (and, therefore, as a manifestation of God's presence in the world)? How have I experienced the opposite, that is, the use of technology for unjust purposes—for the destruction of any part of God's creation? All are asked to focus on the awesomeness of technological advances and to give but one example for each question. The Tuner should be sure to encourage the members of the group to find examples of how technology has touched them directly and personally for good or ill. After the sharing, the group spends some time in shared prayer.

Session IV

The prayer of Jesus at the Last Supper (John 17) was that his followers—indeed all people—might come to a unity that could be likened to the unity that exists between the Father and the Son. It is probably understating the case to say that if such a unity existed among the peoples of the earth, injustice would be wiped out and we would experience "a new heaven and a new earth" (Rev. 21:1–5). Our awareness of what that kind of unity could be often finds its origin in our sense of solidarity with family or community. The sharing in Session IV takes three levels of family as its topic.

Since this sharing will be more about human relationships than that of the two previous sessions, this session should last for a longer period of time in order to give each person more time to relate faith experiences. There are many Scripture passages that can be used to begin the reflection for this period of sharing— among them, Genesis 12:1–3 and 17:1–8, Ezekiel 37:1–14, Luke 10:29–37 and 15:11–32, John 17:20–26, and Revelation 21:1–5.

In their reflections, and in the sharing that will follow, the participants are asked to concentrate on their experience of solidarity with family, with a community (either civic or religious), and with all people of the world. The question is: How have I felt "at one" with my family, with a small, local community, and with the human family, or the world community? All should be asked to deal with each level, even if their experience of one or another of those levels is limited. To take all three areas of experience is important for what will follow, and it has a great deal to do with how we are able to project justice in the world.

It is likely that people will want to pray together at the end of this session. The Tuner should encourage (and even schedule in, if possible) an hour of individual prayer as a "period of synthesis"— a time for each to pull together for themselves all that has been shared during Sessions I to IV.

Session V

The fifth session is intended to reap the fruit of the "period of synthesis." It is to be a communal synthesis of what has been shared, with a view to seeing, perhaps a bit more clearly, what the connection might be between what we believe as Christians and the way we do justice in our world.

In a sense, this is a less formal kind of sharing, and since it could include a bit of discussion, it will probably require more work from the Tuner in keeping the talk focused. One good way of conducting this session is to have it be part of the liturgy of the word at a eucharistic celebration. Three readings are recommended for this liturgy: Genesis 1:26—2:3, Section 27 of Vatican II's Pastoral Constitution on the Church in the Modern World (*Gaudium et Spes*), and Matthew 25:31-46. The dialogue to follow these readings would flow from the questions: How are the experiences shared in the first four sessions connected with the reality of my faith in Jesus? Is there a way I can see now that this faith is, in truth, a call to do justice? (It would be good to explain this session and the questions for sharing before the participants do the hour of personal prayer, that is, at the end of Session IV.)

Whether the sharing is done as part of the liturgy of the word, or separately from the Eucharist, the Tuner should be sure that both (the sharing and the liturgy) remain part of this Faith Experience.

Session VI

Once we have looked at our dignity as human persons, at our experience of justice and injustice, and at how we relate to nature, technology, and the human family, what remains is for us to look at the future and at the possibilities for response as adult Christians in a world so badly in need of people who project justice. Session VI is the first part of that process, and it (like all previous sessions) involves looking at and sharing past experiences. The question is a simple one, but one that goes to the depth of who we are: How have I experienced *conversion* in my life?

The participants should be asked to consider one significant experience of conversion and to explain the significance as they recount the experience. The story of the woman at the well (Jn. 4:7–42), the cure of the man born blind (Jn. 9), the account of the disciples on the road to Emmaus (Lk. 24), or any of the accounts of conversion in the Acts of the Apostles could be read to set the tone for this faith sharing.

A short period of prayer can follow the sharing, or the group can move right into Session VII. The Tuner should assess the atmosphere within the group to determine whether or not a period of prayer is called for. It often happens that when people are sharing at that level (deeply personal) a time of quiet is needed—to let things sink in, and to show respect for the sacredness of what has been shared.

Session VII

In issuing his "call to action" to all Christians, Pope Paul VI wrote:

> It is too easy to throw back on others responsibility for injustices, if at the same time one does not realize how each one shares in it personally, and how personal conversion is needed first. This basic humility will rid action of all inflexibility and sectarianism; it will also avoid discouragement in the face of a task which seems limitless in size. (OA 48)

The final period of sharing in this Faith Experience is one in which the participants are asked to consider their own lives, their faith in Jesus Christ, and their sense of participation in the mission of the Church, and to ask themselves: Where do I need conversion in my life in order to be more of a person who lives like my master, Jesus the Liberator? How could I be one who does justice because of what I believe about Jesus Christ?

If the group is planning a liturgy to bring Faith Experience V to an end, this session could be incorporated either into the penitential rite or into the prayer of the faithful. As usual, the session should include a reading from Scripture (any of the Scripture passages suggested for Session VI would also apply here), time for silent reflection, and the sharing itself. The variation in this session is the response and support of the community. We do not do justice on our own, isolated. Nor do we experience conversion by ourselves. We need each other to grow and to change and to be faithful to the message and call of Jesus.

One way of structuring this session is to invite each person to share his or her need for conversion with the agreement that the person to the right of the speaker will offer, in the name of the community, a prayer in support of the grace of conversion sought by that person. The rest of the community would then be free to add their prayers for this individual. The procedure would be repeated for each person in the group. (Other ways of doing this could be devised by the group or by the Tuner. What should be preserved is the opportunity for each to share and for the community to respond to each person.) A short period of prayer—or the rest of the liturgy—would bring this session (and the entire Faith Experience) to an end.

Obviously, this Faith Experience is simply a beginning. The integration of faith and justice, the understanding of the link between the two, and the living out of this ideal of adult Christianity, in a sense, are lifelong projects. Hopefully, the kind of reflection and sharing encouraged by Faith Experience V will be a help to those who are searching for ways of participating, as Christians, in the transformation of the world.

The following is a synopsis of Faith Experience V (Faith and Justice) as it fits into a weekend schedule.

SESSION I

Friday Evening—7:30–9:30

(a) The Tuner invites the participants to introduce themselves to one another (if necessary), gives a short introduction to faith sharing, and sets down some basic guidelines for the weekend. A brief overview of how this topic, Faith and Justice, will be looked at would probably be helpful to the group at this time.

(b) The Tuner then sets the tone for the first exercise.

(c) Faith Sharing: (1) Fifteen minutes of personal prayer and reflection on the following questions: How have I come to experience my own dignity as a human being? How have I experienced injustice in my life (as agent or victim)? How have I experienced justice in my life (as agent or beneficiary)? (2) Faith sharing on these questions. (3) End with a short period of shared prayer.

SESSION II

Saturday Morning—9:00–10:30

(a) The Tuner reads a passage from Scripture to set the tone for the sharing (e.g., Gen. 1 or Ps. 104 or Mt. 6:25–33) and explains what the topic for sharing will be.

(b) Fifteen minutes of silent prayer and reflection on the question: What are two or three experiences of nature that I have had that became for me real experiences of God? (or What are two or three examples of how I have found God in nature?)

(c) Faith sharing.

(d) A brief period of prayer.

SESSION III

Saturday Morning—11:00–12:30

(a) The Tuner reads a passage from Scripture to set the tone for this session (e.g., Ps. 8, Eccl. 17:3–10, Is. 32:1–8, Is. 2:1–11) and explains the topic for sharing.

(b) Fifteen minutes of silent prayer and reflection on the questions: How have I experienced technology as a force for justice (and, therefore, as a manifestation of God's presence in the world)? How have I experienced the opposite, that is, the use of technology for unjust purposes?

(c) Faith sharing.

(d) Shared prayer.

SESSION IV

Saturday Afternoon—2:00–4:30

(a) The Tuner sets the tone for the sharing with a reading from Scripture (e.g., Gen. 17:1–8, Ez. 37:1–14, Lk. 10:29–37, Lk. 15:11–32, Jn. 17:20–26, Rev. 21:1–5) and explains the session.

(b) Fifteen minutes of silent prayer and reflection on the question: How have I felt "at one" with my family, with a small, local community, and with the human family, or the world community?

(c) Faith sharing on the question.

(d) Shared prayer.

(e) The Tuner should, at the end of this session, explain the questions for the evening session, and ask the participants to spend an hour, from 5:00 to 6:00, in a personal "period of synthesis."

SESSION V

Saturday Evening—7:30–9:30

(a) If this sharing is taking place during the liturgy of the word, the group listens to the readings (Gen. 1:26—2:3, Section 27 of *Gaudium et Spes,* and Mt. 25:31–46), and the Tuner re-explains the topic for sharing. If there is to be no liturgy, one or another of the readings could be used to set the tone for the session.

(b) Faith sharing on the questions: How are the experiences shared in the first four sessions connected to the reality of my faith in Jesus? Is there a way I can see now that this faith is, in truth, a call to do justice? (Since this was the subject of the period of synthesis earlier in the day, there is no need to give fifteen minutes of silence before the sharing.)

(c) Eucharist.

SESSION VI

Sunday Morning—9:00–10:15

(a) The Tuner sets the tone for this session with a Scripture passage (e.g., Jn. 4:7–42, Jn. 9, Lk. 24:13–35) and explains the session.

(b) Fifteen minutes of silent prayer and reflection on the question: How have I experienced conversion in my life? (What is one significant experience of conversion in my life that I would like to share with the group?)

(c) Faith sharing.

(d) Shared prayer.

SESSION VII

Sunday Morning—10:30–12:30

(a) This session can also be part of a closing eucharistic liturgy—either as part of the penitential rite, or as part of the prayer of the faithful. Any of the readings suggested for Session VI can be used here to set the tone for the sharing that will take place.

(b) After the Tuner has explained the session, the group spends fifteen minutes reflecting and praying about: Where do I need conversion in my life in order to be more of a person who lives like my master, Jesus the Liberator? How could I be one who does justice because of what I believe about Jesus Christ?

(c) The sharing takes place in this manner: One person shares his or her need for conversion; the person to the right of the one sharing offers, in the name of the community, a prayer in support of the grace of conversion sought by that person; the rest of the community is then free to offer prayers for that individual. The procedure is repeated for each person in the group.

(d) The session ends with a common prayer (or with the eucharistic liturgy).

6

Faith Experience VI

LIFESTYLE

Now before the feast of the Passover, when Jesus knew that his hour had come to depart out of this world to the Father, having loved his own who were in the world, he loved them to the end. And during supper, Jesus . . . laid aside his garments, and girded himself with a towel. Then he poured water into a basin, and began to wash the disciples' feet, and to wipe them with the towel with which he was girded. . . . When he had washed their feet, and taken his garments, and resumed his place, he said to them, "Do you know what I have done to you? You call me Teacher and Lord; and you are right, for so I am. If I then, your Lord and Teacher, have washed your feet, you also ought to wash one another's feet. For I have given you an example, that you also should do as I have done to you."

Jn. 13:1–15

Lifestyle is an element of our faith that never, until recently, seemed to have any significance at all. We were taught that the way people lived was a matter of choice (and, probably, of fortune) and that this was totally separate from whether or not one lived a good Christian life. We were taught that you could be rich or poor and still be a good Christian—and that, on the whole, it would seem more advantageous to have more than less. There wasn't a great deal of reflecting about all this, nor did we tend to question the truth of the matter.

The question, however, is a live one now for many people. Lifestyle is a real issue in our world, and a real issue for us Christians. And the truth of it is most difficult to uncover. There seems to be no satisfactory answer to approach or implementation. Perhaps there never will be one answer or formula for lifestyle applicable to all people.

126

This chapter proposes one approach to dealing with the question, based on the belief that living out the implications of Christianity—as a people, a Church, called to the values of the Beatitudes and desirous of liberating all peoples—demands "style." What we suggest involves looking at Christianity as a radical approach to living, at climates in which we live, and at "style" as a form of Gospel proclamation. In addition to a Faith Experience format, this chapter will also include a suggested format for keeping a "lifestyle journal."

The journal and some of the basic ideas about approach to lifestyle are the inspiration and the work of a group of Christian Life Community members who met in St. Louis in the summer of 1978 to grapple with this important question. That group included: Barbara Bedolla, Columbia, Md.; Pat and Mike Carter, St. Louis, Mo.; Peter Conk, San Jose, Cal.; Nanette and Jim Ford, St. Louis, Mo.; Molly Fumia, Los Gatos, Cal.; Bob Hawking, Omaha, Neb.; Katherine Oven, Monterey, Cal.; Denise Priestley, Santa Clara, Cal.; Maryanne Rouse, Omaha, Neb.; Paul Roy, S.J., St. Louis, Mo.; Greg Stevens, St. Louis, Mo.; and Paul Thompson, Mountain View, Cal.

CHRISTIANITY: A RADICAL APPROACH TO LIVING

Jesus wanted his followers to be recognizable in this world. He wanted a distinguished band of men and women—a group of outstanding, alive people, who would season life and bring it light and keep its course aimed in the direction of its source: a God one could call Father and regard as the fullness of life itself. You are salt for the earth and light for the world, he would tell them, and you must love one another in the same way that I have loved you (Mt. 5:13–16; Jn. 15:12–13). "A new commandment I give to you, that you love one another; even as I have loved you, so must you also love one another. By this all men will know that you are my disciples, if you have love for one another" (Jn. 13:34–35).

In fact, the way Jesus lived was a radical departure from what was expected of the Jews of his day. He interpreted the law, for example, according to a new criterion: spirit rather than letter, and the spirit of love at that. He called all who would follow him to live with their hearts: truly, it is not right to kill—and more than that, it is not right for you to harbor in your heart any kind of hatred for your brothers and sisters; truly, it is not right to commit adultery—and more than that, it is not right to destroy, even in your heart, what is sacred to another person; truly, it is not right to swear falsely—and more than that, you must be honest with all people, in all situations; truly, you must love your neighbor—and more than that, you must not be vengeful, but forgiving, and your heart must accept friend and enemy. Your love must be such that it will have the power to transform the world. (See Mt. 5:17–48.) The law, for Jesus, was one way for him to live deeply rooted (radically) in the great love God has for all his creation.

Another example of how different, how distinguished, Jesus was is the way he treated humanity. He cherished his fellow human beings and called forth from them power they never even dreamed they had. When a paralytic walked again, it was because he responded to a challenge from Jesus to find that power within himself. In the same way, blind people came to see, the dead were raised to life, and those possessed by evil spirits found that they could be free. And more than that, Jesus sent his disciples to do the same:

> The seventy returned with joy, saying, "Lord, even the demons are subject to us in your name!" And he said to them, "I saw Satan fall like lightning from heaven. Behold, I have given you authority to tread upon serpents and scorpions, and over all the power of the enemy; and nothing shall hurt you. Nevertheless do not rejoice in this, that the spirits are subject to you; but rejoice that your names are written in heaven." (Lk. 10:17–20)

The belief of Jesus in humanity, in his sisters and brothers, was one way for him to live deeply rooted (radically) in the great faith God has in the human beings he has created.

A third example of how Jesus lived his life differently can be found in the way he acted toward his disciples and what he taught them about how they should act toward each other. I have come to serve, he told them, and I will serve you in whatever way I can. I want to use my power to fill you with life, to nourish you with God's word and with the bread of life. I want to cleanse you from sin and to wash your feet, and I will die, if that is what is necessary, to bring you salvation. And still speaking to those who would be his followers, he said: Be as little children (Mt. 18:1–4); don't lord it over others (Mk. 10:41–45); whoever would be the greatest must be the least among you (Lk. 9:46–48); be a neighbor to all you meet (Lk. 10:29–37); "If I, then, your Lord and Teacher, have washed your feet, you also ought to wash one another's feet" (Jn. 13:14). Being a servant was one way that Jesus had of living deeply rooted (radically) in God's fidelity to the covenant he had made with his people.

Those choices that Jesus made—to love God above all else and love his people, to believe deeply in humanity and call forth from it what is best, and to be servant of all and give up his life for his friends—those choices gave Jesus a lifestyle. In other words, the things he chose made the way he lived—his "style"—different, distinguishable from the style of others around him (e.g., tax collectors, or Pharisees, or lawyers, or centurions).

The values Jesus lived by are those values we considered in the Beatitudes (see Chapter 4). And he always encouraged—challenged—his followers to live by the same values. For us, response to that challenge must include more than simple intellectual assent to the goodness and difference of Jesus' life. Living in the true spirit of Jesus, putting on the mind of Christ, must have a radical effect on the "style" of our lives. Christianity in our day—as in the earliest days of the Church—must be rooted in the difference. To be worthy of its message, Christianity must be recognizable as a "countersign" to contemporary society's values and ways of living:

> I have given them thy word; and the world has hated them because they are not of the world, even as I am not of the world. I do not pray that thou shouldst take them out of the world, but that thou shouldst keep them from the evil one. They are not of the world, even as I am not of the world. Sanctify them in the truth; thy word is truth. As thou didst send me into the world, so I have sent them into the world. And for their sake I consecrate myself, that they also may be consecrated in truth. (Jn. 17:14–19)

CLIMATES

How is it possible to approach the question of lifestyle without getting tangled up inside? A whole gamut of feelings may be stirred when the subject is brought up. Sometimes we may feel the *threat* that accompanies the prospect of "downward mobility." How can we simplify our lifestyle, live as Christianity demands, without giving up our freedom to choose, especially to choose the "good things" that life offers? Sometimes we may feel *guilt* because we enjoy life or have things while so many people are dying for want of food or shelter or work or medicine. How can the little we do make all that much difference when the problem is so big? Sometimes we may feel *selfish*. We want as much as we can get. We would like more than we already have—mostly because we get tired of being careful, tired of trying to do without luxuries or things that make life easier or more pleasant. Sometimes we may want more so that we can do more for those who have less. This is an honest feeling, a *wanting to be of service* matched by the realization that material goods often help us to serve others. And sometimes we may experience a very strong *desire for freedom* from so much of what we have. We imagine ourselves totally free—with no attachments to material goods, with no worries about protecting what we have, with no concern about anything weighing us down and preventing us from wholeheartedly being servants of God's people.

What Jesus did during his lifetime was to call his followers to make *choices* about the way they would live. He created a climate that was to determine the "style" of Christianity in a world where other people created other climates that determined other styles. Our present-day world is much the same. People still create climates that determine styles of living, and most of us are fortunate enough to be able to make choices for ourselves. At least the possibility is there for choosing. One important way of approaching the lifestyle question, then, is to take a good, serious, open look at the climates in which we live, at who creates these climates, and at how they and the choices which surround them have an effect on everybody else in our human family.

We will here focus on only a few examples of styles of living—Christian and worldly—to see where the two stand together and where they are opposed to one another. The real work of lifestyle, however, has to be done by each individual and by groups of people who are willing to look at this together.

The climate that determines our way of life in the United States is a blend of a number of factors. One important one is the need of people to belong and the guarantee of a Constitution that all people do belong. The problem is that our equality as human beings has not always been respected as the basic fact that makes possible such a guarantee. Other conditions have been placed by some on whole groups of people—conditions that have stifled or prevented that need from being filled. It is a fact of our history that the color of one's skin has prevented some from belonging. So have a person's age, sex, level of education, heritage, degree of wealth, and religion.

Living in this kind of climate is exhausting. We find our freedom to choose becoming more and more limited, and the need to belong overwhelms us to the point of compromise. It is in this climate that people get caught up in fads: we come to need the superfluous; we must have this or that thing if our life is to have meaning; we must be exactly like the next person if we are to have the resources necessary to preserve our individuality. And it is not long before this climate breeds "oneupmanship," the "be number one" syndrome that makes of us hoarders of the world's goods, and war-mongers, and destroyers of our environment. Others do the choosing for us, tell us what we need (and what, therefore, we must expend our energy on), and trap us into a system that cares little for any but "good old number one."

In contrast, there is a Christian response to that need to belong. It is one in which totally different values are operative. The climate that Jesus created calls for mutual trust and meekness; it is a climate of community, of sharing the goods of this life, of rejoicing at another's fortune and weeping with one in sorrow. The call is for unity: be one—and forget about being "number one." Here the choices remain ours, and true freedom is preserved in each individual. Our meaning does not come from being just like the next person, nor from what material possessions we are able to amass.

> Do not lay up for yourselves treasures on earth, where moth and rust consume and where thieves break in and steal, but lay up for yourselves treasures in heaven, where neither moth nor rust consumes and where thieves do not break in and steal. For where your treasure is, there will your heart be also. (Mt. 6:19–21)

Closely allied to the question of belonging is the question of belongings. There is a climate that is created around possessions, and around the need—the right—to own things. It is the climate that breeds the desire for control of everything around us, that impresses upon us the urgency to be, at all costs, in total control of ourselves. It is in this ambience that we find the "self-made" man or woman, the "true grit" American; and it is here that we find the epitome of selfishness and of ingratitude toward the Giver of all good gifts.

Jesus wanted his followers to look at possessions differently. He called us to an awareness of how truly gifted we are and how desirable it is for us to allow ourselves to be possessed by the Spirit of God. The climate is a more generous one and it brings with it much more freedom:

> And preach as you go, saying, "The kingdom of heaven is at hand." Heal the sick, raise the dead, cleanse lepers, cast out demons. You received without paying; give without pay." (Mt. 10:7–8)

In this climate, Christians can afford to lose themselves and know that this will lead to being self-possessed:

> A disciple is not above his teacher, nor a servant above his master; it is enough for the disciple to be like his teacher, and the servant like his master.... He who finds his life will lose it, and he who loses his life for my sake will find it. (Mt. 10:24–25, 39)

A third area where climates are created has to do with what we believe about responsibility. We live in a disposable culture; we have been "educated" to the idea that we have a right to be taken care of, and are convinced that things—indeed the whole world—must be available to us, at our beck and call, to meet our every need. In a sense, we become passive in a world that must take on its responsibility not only for our survival, but for our happiness and our pleasure and our every whim. In this climate, there is only one thing that brings the world together—connects it—and that is its "responsibility" to focus on me.

Our lives nowadays are spent in lines. We wait in gasoline lines, and in shopping lines, and in lines for roller coasters at amusement parks. But "time is money" and we don't want to wait; we must be first. We set up a climate that exaggerates the importance of our every convenience, and that isolates us—even at times deadens us to the fact that others wait in lines every day for a bowl of food or a bit of medicine that will keep them alive for yet a little while.

The Christian climate is one born of service and of the sense of responsibility that the individual has toward all of creation. A follower of Jesus lives a life of availability to others. It is a climate of connectedness, in which each person is seen and cherished as a brother or sister, where all have a common dignity, where all are called to be actively responsive to each other's needs. In this climate, joy replaces hedonism, and real happiness is found in the total gift of self for the good and life of others.

> This is my commandment, that you love one another as I have loved you. Greater love has no man than this, that a man lay down his life for his friends. (Jn. 15:12–13)

There is a fourth factor that contributes to the development of style in our lives. It is part of a climate that encourages us to "stand our ground." In this climate we are taught about America as the new chosen people, God's own, who have a clear grasp of the truth. Even as individuals, we come to believe that we are right by virtue of our citizenship. And the climate seeps into our personal and our public lives. It is more important now to be right: we work, and discuss, and even fight "not that the truth might appear, but that we might seem to have the upper hand." Being right is a sign of strength and of God's favor (to those to whom God's favor has vestiges of importance). Being wrong, admitting that we don't have all the answers, or seeking out help in dealing with difficulties is seen as weakness or capitulation. It is un-American.

Jesus seems to have taken for granted all along that very few of us are right all the time, and that even fewer have a total grasp of the truth. He was more interested in seeing his followers willing to leave the ground they were standing on if that would lead to a new vision of God or help them to see their brothers and sisters differently. It was a climate of risk that Jesus created, and a prime example of the effects of response to that climate can be found in the conversion of Zacchaeus (Lk. 19:1–10). For Jesus, it was always more important to be righteous (just) than to be right. In this climate, people were aware of the need to do justice—and action in behalf of justice was not approached as something that would salve consciences or meet personal needs to feel good about feeling good in the face of all the misery of the world.

Obviously, these four areas—belonging, belongings, responsibility and covertibility—do not exhaust the question. They are not the only factors that influence style. Nor is the American way of life to be equated with all that is un-Christian. What is important here is the climates that have been created by beliefs, traditions, political philosophies, circumstances, etc., and that have become determiners of the way we live. The more we become willing to look at these climates, the more we will find ourselves in situations where we can exercise free choice about our own lifestyles. And if the criteria for choices are Gospel values, then our style is more likely to approximate what Jesus believed would make his followers recognizable as such in the world.

A QUESTION OF STYLE

The accompanying chart offers a visual representation of what has been discussed in the previous section on climates. The question is not whether one can totally identify (or fit) on one side or another of that chart. The items chosen—on both sides—represent some very basic attitudes that many find in themselves when they engage in this kind of reflection.

One challenge of Christianity is not only the acceptance of the one side (sharing, giving, detachment, joy, conversion, etc.), but also the rooting out of those elements from the other side (hoarding, selfishness, consumerism, disconnectedness, etc.) that keep Christian lifestyle undistinguished and undistinguishable. (Understand, of course, that the lists on either side of the question can be expanded to reflect experiences that have not been noted in this chapter.)

Two things stand out as being of prime importance in the struggle with lifestyle. One is that Jesus calls us to the struggle within the context of community. The style we adopt has to be the product of personal choices made through the challenging and with the support of a people who share life together. Jesus prayed that his disciples would be one so that the world might know and believe that the Father had really sent him into the world and that his style was life-giving for that world: "May they be so completely one that the world will realize that it was you who sent me and that I have loved them as much as you loved me" (Jn. 17:23). And when Jesus called individuals to radical living, it was always as part of "his company"—following him wherever he went:

> Jesus said to [the rich young man], "If you would be perfect, go, sell what you possess and give to the poor, and you will have treasure in heaven; and come, follow me." (Mt. 19:21)

The fact is that we need each other to be able to live radical Christian lives. Part of the radicalness itself is the willingness to depend on others, to be connected to others, to draw strength from others, to be challenged by others—the willingness to be community. And it is also a simple truth that we can see more clearly, delve

STYLE	CLIMATE (Christian)	FACTOR	CLIMATE (Worldly)	STYLE
Unity Sharing Compassion	Freedom Equality Community Trust Meekness	Need to belong	Discrimination Exclusion Dependence on things Oneupmanship	Hoarding Warrior Destructiveness
Giving Detachment Gratitude	Giftedness Being Possessed Generosity	Right to belongings	Possessing Control	Selfishness Consumerism Ingratitude
Service Joy	Availability Connectedness	Call to responsibility	"Disposable culture" "Be taken care of" Be first Disconnectedness	Callousness Hedonism
Humility Conversion	Be righteous Seek the truth	Convertibility	Be right Seek the upper hand	Pride Standing one's ground

more deeply, understand more completely the reality and demands of Gospel living when we look with other people and when we allow their experiences to shed light on our own.

The second important facet of the struggle is that even the slightest bit of conversion to radical Christian living *does* make a difference in the world. It makes a difference on the personal level and on the societal level. When we make personal choices toward living according to the style of Jesus, we make choices that deepen our humanity. We find perspective in our lives, our hearts focus properly, we act more justly, and peace abides in us:

> Therefore I tell you, do not be anxious about your life, what you shall eat or what you shall drink, nor about your body, what you shall put on. Is not life more than food, and the body more than clothing? ... The Gentiles seek all these things; and your heavenly Father knows that you need them all. But seek first his kingdom and his righteousness, and all these things shall be yours as well. (Mt. 6:25–33)

The personal choices that we make about our lifestyle also have an effect on society. At the very least, if our style is more Christian, more simple, more generous, more just, then the world is that much more Christian, simple, generous and just. But more than this, our lives themselves become proclamations of the Gospel of Jesus Christ. We find ourselves, by the way we live, making Jesus visible to the world, allowing him to draw all people to himself; we become witnesses to the truth of the values by which Jesus lived and through which he was able to give life to the world. Indeed, our own attempts to say what is true will be heard only if we *live* what is true. Who, after all, will listen to the proclamation that the poor are blessed from one who hoards? And who will learn the blessings of peace from one who makes war? And who will live in meekness because of the encouragement of one who only hungers and thirsts for power?

The world is looking for people whose lifestyle makes them recognizable as Christians. Just to see such a person gives hope, refreshes, points to new possibilities for the depths to which humanity is called. We cannot help but remember such people and be affected by them.

Perhaps this is why we remember Mary, the mother of Jesus, so well and why so many lives are touched by this woman. Although little is said of her in Scripture, how much of a sense we can get of her style! It is clear that Mary chose to live rooted in her God and that the choices she made give her life special meaning for today. Her style included *availability:* she was totally devoted to her God, willing to do his will, open to the way he would work through her (see Lk. 1), at the same time that she was available for others around her and aware of their needs (Lk. 1:39–56; Jn. 2:1–11). Mary's style was the *gentleness* of a woman who bore a son and cared for him, and who would accept from that son the motherhood of all people. Her style was *contemplative:* she was a person willing to gaze on the Lord, to ponder events, to take to heart the words spoken to her by her God, and to live in a peace that the world could never give. And finally, *simple justice* was the style of this woman. Mary knew the suffering of the anawim, for she was one of them. She could feel with those who were hungry and oppressed, with the lowly, and cry out for the mercy of God. She was able to recognize that the deepest longings of her people and the loftiest call of her God were the same: that justice be done in the world. In her most eloquent prayer, she could sing:

My soul magnifies the Lord,
and my spirit rejoices in God my Savior,
for he has regarded the low estate of his handmaiden.
For behold, henceforth all generations will call me blessed;
for he who is mighty has done great things for me,
and holy is his name.
And his mercy is on those who fear him
from generation to generation.
He has shown strength with his arm,
he has scattered the proud in the imagination of their hearts,
he has put down the mighty from their thrones,
and exalted those of low degree;
he has filled the hungry with good things,
and the rich he has sent empty away.
He has helped his servant, Israel, in remembrance of his
    mercy,
as he spoke to our fathers,
to Abraham and to his posterity forever.

Lk. 1:46–55

This style is unmistakable. In her availability and gentleness, in her simplicity and justice, and in her ability to contemplate God and his universe, Mary truly does become a strong countersign to the world's values, an outstanding evangelizer, and a significant model for us who are seeking to live in the Spirit of Jesus.

It is a question of style, after all. Jesus has called to himself a group of men and women whose personal life choices would be such that they would become visible to all the world—the sight of whom would speak volumes about what is important, about who God really is, and about the greatness that humanity can achieve.

> You are the light of the world. A city set on a hill cannot be hid. Nor do men light a lamp and put it under a bushel, but on a stand, and it gives light to all in the house. Let your light so shine before men, that they may see your good works and give glory to your Father who is in heaven. (Mt. 5:14–16)

Talk about Christian lifestyle is more often than not taken as a threat to much of what we hold dear in our lives. It is sometimes received as an attempt to take away our freedom to choose. Or it is heard as the assertions of a small group of people about what we need or don't need. It is even, at times, interpreted as a scheme to "lay guilt trips" on people if they enjoy themselves, or don't eat the "right" foods, or live in certain types of houses, or drive particular makes of cars.

Somehow we Christians must come to grips with some very basic truths about the man we profess to believe in and to follow. It is true that Christianity demands simplicity and sharing of goods, that it requires unity among people, that it identifies with the poor, that its values are beatitude values, that it seeks to be servant of all, and that it calls us strongly to be public liberators. It is also true that Christianity cannot tolerate hoarding or selfishness in any form, that the spirit of consumerism runs counter to the very spirit of Jesus, that disregard for the fate of the oppressed, or participation in injustice of any kind, is unequivocally un-Christian. And if these are truths, then we must learn to make very basic choices about how we will live in the world and about whether or not we will proclaim the Gospel as true evangelizers.

> Therefore . . . lead a life worthy of the calling to which you have been called. . . . You must no longer live as the Gentiles do, in the futility of their minds; they are darkened in their understanding, alienated from the life of God because

of the ignorance that is in them, due to their hardness of heart; they have become callous and have given themselves up to licentiousness, greedy to practice every kind of uncleanness. You did not so learn Christ—assuming that you have heard about him and were taught in him, as the truth is in Jesus. Put off your old nature which belongs to your former manner of life and is corrupt through deceitful lusts, and be renewed in the spirit of your minds, and put on a new nature, created after the likeness of God in true righteousness and holiness. (Eph. 4:1, 17–24)

FAITH EXPERIENCE VI

Faith Experience VI is different from all of the other faith sharing formats because, while it respects the individual's perception and experience of lifestyle and of the factors that contribute to the development of "style," it is set up to reap the greatest benefit from the way the community—as community—can come to new awarenesses through sharing and mutual challenge and support. Faith Experience VI is a beginning experience of "approaching the question of lifestyle" and requires an explicit agreement from all who participate that they give each other permission to challenge one another. It requires a spirit of adventure, because more than any of the previous Faith Experiences, it leads to the possibility of immediate, real change in the way we live our lives. It requires patience, because the question is so difficult to grasp, and openness, because it more often than not touches many things deep within us and stirs many emotions—some of which are difficult to acknowledge even to ourselves, let alone to a group of people.

There are seven sessions in Faith Experience VI (including two liturgies). Some of these sessions will require Bibles for each participant; others will require newsprint, magic markers, and masking tape for each small group. The Tuner should see to it that these materials are available at the beginning of the faith sharing.

Session I

As at the beginning of all Faith Experiences, the Tuner should be sure that all of the participants have been introduced to each other and that all are familiar with (and agree to) the basic ground rules for faith sharing. It is generally helpful for all to have a chance to voice their expectations and to say briefly how they feel as they begin this time of sharing. The Tuner should then give a quick overview of Faith Experience VI, noting that newsprint will be used at many of the sessions and that part of this Faith Experience involves group discussion, synthesis and strategizing. These are activities that have not been part of previous faith sharing formats.

After these preliminaries, the Tuner explains the first session and leads the group in it. This is intended to be a prayerful, reflective sharing that will probably influence the sharing in Sessions II to VII. There are five basic steps to follow for Session I. First, the Tuner sets the tone for the sharing by reading a passage from Scripture and offering a prayer for the Lord's inspiration and blessing on the group. Luke 10:21–24, Mark 7:1–8, and Matthew 13:1–9 are appropriate for this. Next, at the Tuner's invitation, the group spends a half hour in silent prayer and reflection on the question: What are three things in the Gospel that to my mind cannot be watered down? Participants should be encouraged to use their Bibles during this time and to write down (briefly) what those three things are for them. In the third step, the participants are asked to share what they have written and a composite list is drawn up and written down on newsprint for all to see. The fourth part of this session is another period of silent prayer and reflection (for five minutes or so) on everything that the group has said about the Gospel. In other words, the newsprint becomes the focus of the prayer. Finally, for as long as the group wishes, there is a period of shared prayer to bring the session to an end.

Session II

The second session establishes a pattern that will be followed in Sessions III, V, and VI. Each of these sessions will include an explanation and tone-setting by the Tuner, a time for personal prayer, faith sharing, and a group synthesis of what has been shared. The progression of the sessions is a movement from Gospel (II) to personal (III) to societal (V) values and then back to personal response to those values (VI).

In Session II, the participants are asked to look at the person of Jesus, to consider his life as the Gospels describe it, and to try to assess the "style" that was characteristic of this man. The thesis here (as for this entire Faith Experience) is that the things we *choose* for ourselves, the decisions we make about how we are going to be, what we are going to do and what we are going to have, are what characterize the style of our lives. And so, the question for reflection and sharing in this session is: What are four things that Jesus chose that describe his lifestyle?

After the Tuner has read an appropriate passage from Scripture (e.g., Jn. 12:20–28, Mt. 5:1–10, Mk. 2:23–38, or Lk. 9:23–27) and explained the session, the participants are invited to spend one hour in personal prayer and reflection on the above question. The group should be asked to write down the four choices of Jesus in order to facilitate the sharing that will take place. During the sharing, someone from the group is asked to set down on newsprint the elements of Jesus' lifestyle that are being spoken about. Once all have had a chance to speak, the group spends an hour or so synthesizing what is on the newsprint with a view to better understanding, communally, what the style of Jesus was and what Jesus might have been saying to us about lifestyle. The main job of the Tuner, at this point, will be to keep the discussion focused on Jesus and his lifestyle. The session closes with a brief period of prayer.

Session III

Session III follows the same steps as Session II, the focus this time shifting to the personal choices and lifestyles of the participants. The question for prayer and sharing is: What are four things that I choose that describe my lifestyle? Scripture passages that might be used to set the tone for this session include Matthew 8:5–13, Mark 2:15–17, Luke 5:33–39, and John 3:25–30.

An important part of the tone-setting that should be done by the Tuner is a brief reflection on the nature of this kind of sharing. The tendency is for us to make value judgments about lifestyles (including our own) before taking the time necessary to identify the elements of the style. Whether a person is rich or poor, for example, is morally neutral, but if we hold up a poor Christ as the example of lifestyle, then it can be perceived as "immoral" to have money. If the sharing is not to be an anxiety or guilt producing time, the participants must be willing to allow for a variety of styles and be willing also to identify their own style just for the sake of identifying it. Looking at that style in light of the Gospel and asking questions about how it might be changed to better reflect Christian values are later steps in the process.

After an hour of prayer on the question (it would be helpful here to ask the participants to write down on newsprint a summary of what they will share) and an hour of sharing, the group should spend another hour looking at the different styles, at how people describe styles differently, and at how what has been shared can help them get a clearer grasp of the lifestyle question. Once again, this is a kind of discussion that can easily get off the primary focus, and the skills of the Tuner are required to prevent this from happening.

If Sessions III and IV are being done on the same day, the group should take a short break after the discussion. If they are being done on different days, the discussion could end with a period of shared prayer.

Session IV

The fourth session is a eucharistic liturgy. It is intended to be a simple celebration—a time of quiet prayer. The participants have looked at Gospel values, at the choices of Jesus, and at their own choices. This liturgy should celebrate those values and choices, as well as the gift of freedom which our God gives to all people and which we are able to exercise in determining the style of our lives. The celebrant should set the proper tone for this celebration and be sure that there is sufficient time for all to be silent and to remember what has been shared and what is real gift from the Lord. Perhaps one or two of the readings mentioned earlier in this chapter could be used during the liturgy of the word; also, the fourth Eucharistic Prayer is one that reflects prayerful remembering.

Session V

Session V goes back to the pattern of Sessions II and III. The Tuner sets the tone for this time of prayer and sharing (Mt. 9:35–38, Mk. 4:21–25, Lk. 8:19–21, or Jn. 10:7–18 can be used here), explains what the focus will be, and invites the people to spend a half hour in prayer. The goal of this session is to look at the lifestyle that has become characteristic of our country. The question for reflection and sharing is: What are four things in this country that describe its lifestyle? (The premise here is that "a people" can develop a particular style that sets them off from other groups and that the style of "the people" is a collection of styles that are more or less lived by the individuals within that group.)

Newsprint should be used in this session, and after all have had a chance to share, a discussion should follow in order to develop a composite picture of the style or styles which are perceived in this country. The discussion should also deal with the climates that are created by our values as a nation and with the ways in which the freedom that was celebrated in Session IV is either helped or stifled by our national lifestyle.

This session should end with a short period of shared prayer.

Session VI

Response, in the area of lifestyle, is a matter of personal choice made in light of values that have acquired significance in the life of the person who is choosing. The ambience of our choices must include more than the country in which we live, more than what the media currently impress upon us as being all-important for our growth and health. The world in which we live, the Gospel faith we profess, and the call we experience from our God must also be elements in the choosing. And while the choices themselves must be personal, the living out of a lifestyle that reflects Christian values will depend greatly on the support that we can get from the Christian community.

Session VI tries to get at both of these sides of response: personal choice and communal support. The important thing in this session is to encourage the reflection while keeping intact the freedom of each individual participant to do something or not at the time of the faith sharing. The questions for reflection have the potential for taking away that freedom. The Tuner must make it clear (and should get an explicit agreement from the group) that no pressure will be exerted on anyone to make any specific response whatsoever.

The questions to be dealt with are the following: (a) What elements of my lifestyle are changeable? (b) Is there anything in my present lifestyle that I could change in order to live a style that more closely embodies Gospel values? (c) How can the community help me to effect and live out this change?

After a reading from Scripture (Mt. 5:13–16, Mk. 6:7–13, Lk. 5:29–32, or Jn. 6:52–69) and a careful explanation of this session, the participants spend an hour praying over these questions, writing on newsprint (if they wish) an outline of what they will share. The sharing takes place and is followed by a time of "discussion and strategizing." It is here that the group looks at what individuals have expressed as possible ways of changing their lifestyle and asks itself: How can we help each other live our Gospel values more deeply? The Tuner should keep the group focused on the concrete

examples of change as the referents for this discussion. At the end
of the discussion, the Tuner should explain what is intended for
Session VII and give the participants time to prepare for it.

Session VII

This final session of Faith Experience VI is a eucharistic liturgy during which individuals will have the opportunity to formalize
a commitment to simplify their lifestyle if they so desire. It is possible that the sharing done in the first six parts of this Faith Experience, especially that of Session VI, has given some of the
participants a fairly clear indication of some concrete action/choice
that could be made with regard to their lifestyle. If this is the case,
then the ceremony of commitment becomes a help to those persons
and gives them the chance to make that commitment before the
Lord. This also becomes the occasion for the entire community to
formally confirm the choices and to commit itself to support the individuals in the decisions they are making.

The ceremony of commitment can be held as a response to the
liturgy of the word (Eph. 4:11–24, Ps. 15, and Mt. 6:25–33 are recommended for this liturgy) or just before the kiss of peace. The following is an example of the kind of "formula" that could be written
for this ceremony:

Individual:

> I stand before the Lord and before this
> Christian community, aware of the freedom
> I have to decide what my lifestyle will be.
> I want my life to reflect more and more the
> values of Jesus and of his Gospel. And so
> I make the following commitment: I choose . . .
>
> This is a commitment that I make with joy
> and with great hope. I pray that the Lord
> will bless me in this choice, and I pray, too,
> that this community will help me live it out.

Community:

> We, your community, affirm you in this choice. We share
> your joy and your hope. And we commit ourselves to do

whatever we can to help you be faithful to what you have chosen. May the Lord's blessing and peace be with all of us.

All:

Amen.

We end somewhat as we began. Faith Experience VI is a different kind of faith sharing. It is a beginning approach to a very perplexing question and undoubtedly the most taxing of the Faith Experiences. And yet, it is the most challenging because it opens for each of us the possibility of prophetic participation in justice. Ultimately it is our style as a Christian people that will proclaim the liberating presence of the Lord in the midst of his people. Ultimately it is our style as a Christian people that will stand as a countersign to the death-dealing "values" of our world. And ultimately it is our style as a Christian people that will reverse the lifestyle process and itself create a new climate on our planet, a climate characteristic of the kingdom of which we are all a part: the kingdom of life and truth, the kingdom of holiness and grace, the kingdom of justice, love and peace.

The following is a synopsis of Faith Experience VI (Lifestyle) as it fits into a weekend schedule.

SESSION I

Friday Evening—7:30–9:30

(a) The Tuner gives a short introduction to faith sharing and sets down some basic guidelines for the weekend.

(b) The Tuner sets the tone for the first session.

(c) Initial sharing: (1) The Tuner reads a passage from Scripture (e.g., Lk. 10:21–24, Mk. 7:1–8, or Mt. 13:1–9). (2) Thirty minutes of personal prayer and reflection on the question: What are three things in the Gospel that, to my mind, cannot be watered down? (3) Sharing and writing on newsprint a composite list of what is shared. (4) Five minutes of prayer on what has been shared. (5) Shared prayer.

SESSION II

Saturday Morning—9:00–12:00

(a) The Tuner reads a passage from Scripture (e.g., Jn. 12:20–28 or Mt. 5:1–10) and explains the session.

(b) One hour of personal prayer on the question: What are four things Jesus chose that describe his lifestyle?

(c) Faith sharing on the above question. Newsprint is used to write down what is being shared.

(d) Group synthesis of what has been shared: What was the style of Jesus?

(e) Shared prayer.

SESSION III

Saturday Afternoon—1:00–5:00

(a) The Tuner sets the tone for this session (Mt. 8:5–13 or Mk. 2:15–17) and explains the session.

(b) One hour of personal prayer on the question: What are four things I choose that describe my lifestyle? (Have participants write choices on newsprint.)

(c) Faith sharing on the above question.

(d) Group discussion on the question of lifestyle.

(e) Shared prayer.

SESSION IV

Saturday Afternoon—5:15

A simple eucharistic liturgy celebrating the gift of freedom that God gives to all and that we are able to exercise in determining the style of our lives. It is recommended that the homily be replaced by—or set the tone for—a period of prayerful remembering of what has been shared.

SESSION V

Saturday Evening—7:30–9:30

(a) The Tuner sets the tone for the sharing session (e.g., Jn. 10:7–18 or Lk. 8:19–21) and explains the session.

(b) Thirty minutes of personal prayer on the question: What are four things in this country that describe its lifestyle?

(c) Faith sharing and a drawing up, on newsprint, of a composite picture of our national lifestyle.

(d) Group synthesis and discussion of the above.

(e) Shared prayer.

SESSION VI

Sunday Morning—9:00–12:00

(a) The Tuner sets the tone for this exercise (e.g., Mk. 6:7–13 or Jn. 6:52–69) and explains the questions for prayer and sharing.

(b) One hour of personal prayer on the questions: What elements of my lifestyle are changeable? Is there anything in my present lifestyle that I could change in order to live a style that more closely embodies Gospel values? How can the community help me to effect and live out this change? (The participants should be asked to write out their reflections on newsprint.)

(c) Faith sharing.

(d) Group discussion on how the community can help its members make choices about Gospel lifestyle.

(e) The Tuner gives an explanation of the ceremony of commitment that will be in Session VII.

SESSION VII

Sunday Afternoon—12:30

This session is a closing eucharistic liturgy. The participants are given an opportunity to make a commitment to change their lifestyle in some way if they wish to do so. The ceremony of commitment, which includes individuals' choices and the promise of support from the community, can be held as a response to the liturgy of the word or before the kiss of peace. The Scripture passages recommended for this liturgy are Ephesians 4:11–24, Psalm 15, and Matthew 6:25–33.

LIFESTYLE JOURNAL

There are three parts to this journal: (a) a personal inventory to be taken at the beginning of the journalizing, (b) questions for daily reflection, and (c) a weekly review. What is presented here is a set of guidelines that are certainly not all-inclusive. They should be refined in such a way as will help you get into the spirit of this kind of reflection.

A. Personal Inventory

1. What do I own?
   - individually and collectively
   - all material possessions owned
   - specific number of items (e.g., articles of clothing)
   - monetary value
   - money in the bank
   - salary
   - money given to charity

2. Where do I live?
   - geographic location
   - who lives around me?
   - what ethnic groups?
   - property value of neighborhood

3. Who are my friends?
   - what do they own?
   - where do they live?

4. What do I spend most of my time doing?
   - make a "pie" of your life
   - set up a priority list e.g., career
     reading
     TV

After taking the personal inventory:
Does all of this say anything about me? to me?

B. Daily Reflection

What do I spend most of my time doing?

(Note: All of these questions are for reflection. You will perhaps choose different ones to write about each day.)

1. Make a "pie" of each day
   - How did I spend my time today?
   - How much time with my spouse? children? friends? community?
   - How was this time spent?

2. What did I spend money on today?
   - bare necessities
   - extras

3. What did food have to do with my day?

4. Did I feel any strong emotions today?
   - anger? joy? loneliness? love? etc.
   - what made me feel these?
   - did I share these feelings with someone?
   - why? why not?

5. Did I make myself aware of how my life affects others?

6. Was I challenged by anyone or anything today?

7. Did I challenge anyone?

8. Did I affirm anyone? Was I affirmed?

9. How do I feel about the way I spent my day?

10. Is there anything else I want to say?

C. Weekly Review

When was I doing my ministry the best this week?

7

PERSONAL AND COMMUNAL REFLECTION

Full authority has been given to me both in heaven and on earth; go, therefore, and make disciples of all nations. Baptize them in the name of the Father, and of the Son, and of the Holy Spirit. Teach them to carry out everything I have commanded you. And know that I am with you always, until the end of the world.

Mt. 28:18–20

Our lives must be lived trying to remember this great promise of our God—that he will be with us for all time. It's not always that clear—nor is it always easy to remember. The Faith Experience formats described in the first six chapters are examples of how we can help each other to remember and to focus on that dynamic presence of the Lord. This chapter looks at faith sharing as a way to spirituality, and at how prayer is the connecting element between the remembering in faith that we do and the living in faith that we strive for. This will be followed by an explanation of a prayer/faith-sharing format that can be used at regular gatherings of a Christian community.

LIFE EXPERIENCES/FAITH EXPERIENCES

Most of us would be quick to admit that our lives are quite ordinary. We experience pretty much the same kinds of things that other people do; we are aware of some outstanding moments, of times which bring the depth of life to our consciousness, but for the most part life is simple and unsensational. And perhaps it is this ordinary-ness that most of us are content to bring to our relationship with God. Mysticism is, after all, for mystics. Deep experiences of prayer are for special people (read: for others, not us). And life-shaking experiences of faith belong to the likes of St. Peter or St. Paul or St. Ignatius. If this is true, then we run the risk of living lives devoid of enthusiasm for life itself—lives that will never know, on this earth at least, what it means to befriend God.

Faith is that which places us where we can perceive life differently, that is, on the level of the extraordinary. Our faith experiences are, in reality, the ordinary experiences of our lives looked at—reflected upon—in the light of our belief that God is somehow to be found there. Faith is that willingness to live life in the belief that God is present. It is a willingness to let the ordinary-ness of life become transparent so that the extraordinary beauty of God's very life within it might shine through. When this happens, we can affirm the goodness of creation and know the wonder of our participation in it. Our faith experiences are, in reality, our experiences of the transfiguration of all of reality, of our whole world, of our own lives—after the likeness of Christ.

> And after six days Jesus took with him Peter and James and John his brother, and led them up a high mountain apart. And he was transfigured before them, and his face shone like the sun, and his garments became white as light. And behold, there appeared to them Moses and Elijah, talking with him. And Peter said to Jesus, "Lord, it is well that we are here; if you wish, I will make three booths here, one for you and one for Moses and one for Elijah." He was still speaking, when lo, a bright cloud overshadowed them, and a voice from the cloud said, "This is my beloved Son, with whom I am well pleased; listen to him." When the disciples heard this, they fell on their faces, and were filled with awe. But Jesus came and touched them, saying, "Rise, and have no fear." And when they lifted up their eyes, they saw no one but Jesus only. (Mt. 17:1–8)

I believe that the gift of faith is that which makes possible our enjoyment of this world. It is this gift which "betrays" us as Christians—as followers of the one who came to give us joy (Jn. 15:11), to show us the face of God (Jn. 14:9), and to root us in spirited living (Jn. 16:12–15). When we live by faith, we filter our life experiences through that tremendous gift and allow ourselves to be totally influenced by the Spirit of the risen and glorified Jesus. When we live by faith, we let the Holy Spirit beget spirit within us and we experience life in a new way—as newborn children of God:

> That which is born of the flesh is flesh, and that which is
> born of the Spirit is spirit. Do not marvel that I said to you,
> "You must be born anew." (Jn. 3:6–7)

When we live by faith, we become more able to reach to the heart of the world and to understand its inmost joys and sorrows. Our own hearts acquire depth-perception, and our lives are never quite the same—never, if the truth be told, ordinary.

Spirited living—spirituality—is our human way of being in relationship with our God. It is living with, interacting with, communicating with, growing with and being in love with a person who is believed, on the ordinary level of things, to be impossible to live with, interact with, communicate with, grow with and be in love with. Spirituality is life—human life—begotten of Spirit, transfigured, rendered extraordinary. Yet all the while it remains human and grows in its delightful humanity, and it remains rooted in creation and it continues its yearning for completion in Christ (Rom. 8:19–23).

What I am suggesting in all of this is different from simply giving a religious interpretation to human experience or from superimposing some artificial "spiritual" meaning onto that experience. Real spirituality is a way of living our lives "in touch" with the Spirit of God within us and open to ever new possibilities in our relationship with God. Real spirituality is total involvement of our humanity in the possibility of transfiguration.

PRAYER

In our faith-living—in our growth in spirituality—prayer takes on a new significance. If our focus is on the living out of a real relationship—a human relationship (the only kind we humans are capable of)—with God, then prayer becomes one of a series of moments in that relationship. The question of saying prayers or of "putting in the time" (that magic hour a day) fades in importance. The important thing is to grow in intimacy with our God.

I would like to suggest three aspects of prayer that I believe lead to intimacy with God. They are three essential parts of my definition of prayer. (I must add from the outset that, along with my belief about prayer as a human means of becoming intimate with God, is my deep belief that God cannot be boxed in by us humans. Our God is one who loves us enough to transcend our meager efforts and to gift us with life as he wills, regardless of how "good" or "poor" our prayer might seem to us.)

The first—and most essential—aspect of prayer, for me, is the stance of the psalmist in Psalm 139:

> O Lord, you have probed me and you know me;
> you know when I sit and when I stand;
> you understand my thoughts from afar.
> My journeys and my rest you scrutinize,
> with all my ways you are familiar.
> Even before a word is on my tongue,
> behold, O Lord, you know the whole of it.
> Behind me and before, you hem me in
> and rest your hand upon me.
> Such knowledge is too wonderful for me;
> too lofty for me to attain.
>
> Where can I go from your spirit?
> From your presence where can I flee?
> If I go up to the heavens, you are there;
> if I sink to the nether world, you are present there.
> If I take the wings of the dawn,
> if I settle at the farthest limits of the sea,
> even there your hand shall guide me,
> and your right hand hold me fast.
> If I say, "Surely the darkness shall hide me,
> and night shall be my light"—
> for you darkness itself is not dark,
> and night shines as the day. (Ps. 139:1–12)

There is here a deep realization that one does best by standing in total honesty before God. There is, after all, no place to hide—nor is there any need to hide. I stand before my God as I am—wearing no mask, playing no role, fearing nothing—because I stand before the one who created me, the one who loves me, the one who has redeemed me by the blood of the first-born Son. It is the safest place in the universe.

My experience—personal and vicarious—is that we humans

spend most of our prayer time outside of that "safest place." We project idols of ourselves to our God—adorable little images of us that could withstand even public scrutiny. Or we project caricatures of our sinful selves—horrible creatures who can only cower before an all-powerful being and beg that our due punishment be meted out (albeit with a bit of mercy). Or worse yet, we don't even try to project ourselves at all: "Nothing personal, you know...." We spend much of our prayer time not really believing that God is God, but making believe that we are persons other than who we really are.

I find it helpful to look at other human relationships I am involved in to test the truth of what I believe about my relationship with God. My other relationships also help me to find ways of acting—things to do—that will enhance the relationship. Consider, for example, your best friend—the person you are closest to in the whole world. Is it not true that part of the closeness is due to the fact that this person knows more about you (of you) than anyone else? Aren't you most honest with this person? Don't you find it next to impossible to hide anything from him/her? And once a trust is built, don't you feel "safe" with this person—even knowing all that he/she knows about you? Are you not convinced that your best friend has your very life at heart and wants only what is good for you? Indeed, a best friend is one with whom we can interact—with whom we can be—without fear. To be so intimate is a great blessing.

The beginning of intimate prayer, I believe, is the willingness to accept that God knows us *totally* and that it is impossible to hide from him. We become more willing to freely reveal ourselves in trust. With this comes the realization that God really does love us, everything about us—and we begin to *know* more about God and more about ourselves. The truth of that love casts out whatever fear could stand in the way of the deep relationship that is possible between God and a human being.

So, to the degree that we stand before God in honesty, to that degree do we allow the possibility of intimate prayer to take place. And to the degree that we stand before God as who we are, to that degree do we become present to him and allow him to be present to us.

Presence is the second important aspect of prayer. It is that quality of *being with* a person that comes from honesty and that leads to mutual self-gifting. When two people are really present to each other, they reach a depth of relationship that goes beyond any word that could be said or any gift that could be given. For, at that moment, the two give themselves to each other. They stand together. They share a "sacred place." So, too, with our God. When we pray in this way, there is no question—indeed, there isn't any possibility—of distractions. It no longer matters that we have nothing to say; in fact, there is sometimes a need to say nothing at all.

Presence, when it is the result of honesty before God, can lead to many different kinds or experiences of prayer. In addition to what we might call the prayer of deep love, where two persons give themselves to each other, this intimate presence can also be a time when the two look together at what is outside of themselves. They can contemplate the beauty of creation or the suffering of humanity, the struggles of the just or the rejoicing of children—and understand these things better because they look together, through each other's eyes. I believe that one of the meanings of the incarnation is that God was seeking this kind of presence with humanity: our God came to look at the world through human eyes—with a human heart—and called us, in Jesus, to reciprocate that presence and challenged us to look at the same world through the eyes and the heart of God. It makes all the difference in the world, and leads us to the third aspect of prayer: response.

The response I am speaking of here is a wholehearted commitment to the love relationship and to the implications of that relationship. It means being willing to "exercise" the honesty and the presence. It means being willing to feel what I feel, to want what I want, to say what is inside me, and to continue believing that it is only this that will deepen the intimacy. Sometimes this will be a question of admitting my own failures and of seeking the Lord's forgiveness. At other times, it will be a question of telling the Lord that we forgive him for . . . whatever—his lack of clarity, his having taken someone from us, his having hurt us, however unintentional the hurt might have been.

Response will also mean a giving over of our lives into the hands of the Lord, or a surrender/dedication of our lives to those whom the Lord loves. Response will mean daring to let the intimacy continue, refusing to be afraid of anything because we believe that our God is a good God, who loves us, who has our very life at heart.

These three—honesty, presence, and response—are what I believe to be basic elements of intimate relationships. They are not presented in chronological order or in order of importance. They are all important and they are interdependent. Each grows because of the others. Each enhances the others. All three help us to become pray-ers—prayerful people—people serious about being in relationship with God. All, therefore, become important elements of spirituality. They become for us instances of our openness to the Holy Spirit, begetting spirit within us and drawing us more deeply, more intimately, into that life of God.

COMMUNAL SPIRITUALITY

The implications of a real spirituality must go beyond the individual and the individual relationship with God. There can be no such thing as private prayer to a God who has chosen to identify with "the public": "Truly, I say to you, as you did it to one of the least of these my brethren, you did it to me" (Mt. 25:40). There can be no such thing as a solitary spirituality for anyone who wants to be truly human, for we are members of a human family, we are one body, with Christ as head:

> For the body does not consist of one member but of many. If the foot should say, "Because I am not a hand, I do not belong to the body," that would not make it any less a part of the body. And if the ear should say, "Because I am not an eye, I do not belong to the body," that would not make it any less a part of the body. If the whole body were an eye, where would be the hearing? If the whole body were an ear, where would be the sense of smell? ... As it is, there are many parts, yet one body. The eye cannot say to the hand, "I have no need of you," nor again the head to the feet, "I have no need of you." ... God has so composed the body ... that there may be no discord in the body, but that the members may have the same care for one another. If one member suffers, all suffer together; if one member is honored, all rejoice together. Now you are the body of Christ and individually members of it. (1 Cor. 12:14–27)

We do, in fact, need each other, and we are called to live as a people, as one human family, as brothers and sisters one to another. The faith sharing of the first six chapters has had as one of its goals to bring together the people of God into a greater unity. By sharing our faith experiences with the people around us, one of the things we do is to identify, or get in touch with, or discover, the Spirit that animates the community. For just as God truly works in the lives of each person, so does he truly work in the life of his people.

I often hear people attest that they get very little from their local church, that a sense of real Christian community is sorely wanting where they live. My belief is that this is because very few local churches (at least in my experience) spend much time seriously seeking out the Spirit that animates them communally. A truly alive Christian community is one that is consciously working at developing a common spirituality—a way, precisely as community, of relating with God. This requires an investment of time, a good deal of hard work, and a lot of risk on the part of many individuals.

Christian community, I believe, is built up through the conscious acceptance of the fact that the Lord is alive in the person I work with, or live with, or play with, or worship with. And this conscious, explicit acceptance cannot come about unless the faith that we hold in common is shared, unless we give real testimony to the working of the Lord in our lives, unless we become willing to proclaim (share) among each other the Contemporary Testament, the good news of salvation in Jesus Christ being worked out in our day.

It happens, also, that when we are willing to share our faith, and our faith experiences, we actually come to share our honesty before God, our presence to him, and our response to the many calls that come to us from the Lord. In other words, we share our intimacy with God with those around us, and a real Christian intimacy is made possible within the community. Then the incredible implications of the mission of Jesus begin to unfold in our midst:

> Now is the judgment of this world, now shall the ruler of this world be cast out; and I, when I am lifted up from the earth, will draw all men to myself. (Jn. 12:31–32)

> I do not pray for these only, but also for those who believe in me through their word, that they may all be one; even as thou, Father, art in me, and I in thee, that they also may be in us, so that the world may believe that thou hast sent me. The glory which thou hast given me I have given to them, that they may be one even as we are one, I in them and thou in me, that they may become perfectly one, so that the world may know that thou hast sent me and hast loved them even as thou hast loved me. Father, I desire they they also, whom thou hast given to me, may be

with me where I am, to behold my glory which thou hast given me in thy love for me before the foundation of the world. (Jn. 17:20–24)

It was the wish, the prayer, the life work of Jesus to bring us to a point where his intimacy with the Father would be ours—with the Father and with all of creation. What a marvelous gift—the gift of perfect love, casting out all fear, bringing all together to the glory of God.

PERSONAL AND COMMUNAL REFLECTION

Our participation in the Faith Experience and in the shared faith of a Christian community, if it brings us to a renewed sense of our need to be in relationship with God, must also bring us to an ever-deepening realization of what seems to me to be one of the great messages of our salvation history as recorded in both the Old and New Testaments, namely, that we live always in the presence of God.

From the time of creation (Gen. 1–3) when God walked in the "garden in the cool of the day" (Gen. 3:3) and through all of salvation history, God's word has been spoken to say to his people: "I am with you."

The message to Moses—even in the name "Yahweh"—was: "I am the One who is with you" (Ex. 3:14). To Isaiah came the promise of "Emmanuel"—God-with-us (Is. 7:14). And in Deutero-Isaiah, Yahweh commands his prophet to comfort his people (Is. 40), to say to them: "Fear not, for I am with you" (Is. 41:10), because "you are precious in my eyes, and honored, and I love you. . . ." (Is. 43:4–5). When Jeremiah protested his vocation, God's answer was, "Be not afraid of them, for I am with you to deliver you" (Jer. 1:8). And when the angel Gabriel appeared to Mary, he said, "Hail, O favored one; the Lord is with you" (Lk. 1:28).

God's most telling word of salvation—spoken in the New Testament to announce our salvation once and for all—is Jesus, God with us, our salvation itself enfleshed. It is significant that the last words spoken by Jesus to his disciples (Mt. 28:20) are: "Know that I am with you always, until the end of the world."

One of the tremendous implications of the kind of lives we are all trying to live is that we must be permeated with this sense of the presence of God. We do not just occasionally "place ourselves in the presence of God." We *are*—always—in his presence. Our way of living in relationship with God—our spirituality—calls us to be "contemplatives in action." This does not mean that our actions are to become our prayer, but that we are to be so caught up with the realization that we live in God's presence that all of our actions can be carried out under the influence of and with an ever-increasing consciousness of that presence.

The "examen of consciousness," as it is explained by George Aschenbrenner, S.J., in an article which appeared in the January 1972 issue of *Review for Religious,* is really a time that we set aside each day, in prayer, to reflect specifically on how we have grown in our awareness—our consciousness—of the presence of God as we went about doing whatever we were doing. Fr. Aschenbrenner suggests that this daily exercise of personal discernment is possible through prayerful personal reflection on our consciousness of God's presence and activity in our lives. The reflection is based on the examen prescribed by St. Ignatius in the Spiritual Exercises, and the following are suggestions as to how this kind of examen may be used both by individuals (personal reflection) and by communities (communal reflection).

PERSONAL REFLECTION

In the Spiritual Exercises of St. Ignatius, the examen contains five basic points. It is important to remember, as we look at these points, that the examen is a time of prayer, and that the real goal of this prayer, as of any other prayer, is a deepening of our life with God, a growing awareness of the calls of God to us, a more loving response to those calls, that in the end God might be truly "all in all," recognized and acclaimed by the entire universe as the Lord and Master of creation.

The first point of the examen is *thanksgiving*. I begin my personal reflection with a prayer of thanks to God for all of the favors, graces, blessings, and gifts received during the day. It is within this context that I meet my God—he is the giver of all good gifts, and I most clearly experience his presence in my life through the many good things that happen to me because of his great goodness to me. And so I give thanks.

The second point is *petition*. I pause for a moment to reflect on the grace I seek during this time of prayer—the grace to see where I have failed to respond to God's love, the grace to free myself from my sins, the grace to recognize areas in my life which need growth, the grace to recognize those times when I have, indeed, been faithful and responsive to the promptings of the Spirit.

The third point is *reflection*. Ignatius uses the term "to demand an account of my soul." This is the part of the prayer during which I actually look over the past day. I make a review, in the light of my gratitude to God for his gifts, and in light also of the particular grace I have just sought. Again, the goal must be prayer leading to depth, not morbid introspection or "guilt-tripping."

In the fourth point, I *ask pardon* for my faults. If the main emphasis of the reflection was on my failure to respond, then I seek forgiveness and reconciliation. If the emphasis was on responses that I was able to make, then I again thank God for his goodness and pray that I may be able to continue growing in my love for him and in my service of him.

The fifth point is a *resolution of amendment*. It is here that I express my desires for growth, that I seek to be more faithful, that I speak to the Lord of the way I really want to live my life.

Through the use of this form of prayer, as Fr. Aschenbrenner points out, I can become more adept at recognizing God alive in me, calling me to a fuller life of love and service for him and for his people.

One further observation about personal reflection. If I am praying in this way in order to be more discerning about the activity of God in and through my life, it is also helpful to keep a daily journal of reflections. The idea here is not to keep a diary of my activities, but simply to spend five or ten minutes at the end of each day recording my experience with regard to my relationship with God. With these kinds of reflections written down, it becomes perhaps a bit easier, over a period of two weeks or a month, to identify what might be termed a "gradual calling" from the Lord. (Ideally, of course, I would have a guide—a spiritual director—with whom I could share these things and who could help me integrate them into my life.)

COMMUNAL REFLECTION

Taking the basic insight of St. Ignatius about the value of regular personal reflection, it is possible to develop a prayer format based on the Ignatian examen that would allow a community to become involved in what we call "communal reflection." Once again, there are five steps to this prayer, and the goal is a deepened awareness of the presence of God.

First, there is a *call to presence*. The Tuner, or the prayer leader, simply invites the community to recall God's presence, here and now, as the group gathers in the name of Jesus. A short passage from Scripture may be read in order to help the individuals in the group to quiet themselves and to attend to that presence.

There follows a period of *personal reflection*. For five or ten minutes, the members of the community silently look back over the period of time since their last meeting to consider those times when they experienced God's presence (or absence) in their lives. Different questions may be formulated to focus this reflection and the sharing that follows. A number of these questions are given as examples at the end of this chapter.

The third step is a time of *faith sharing*. The group is now invited to share some of those experiences they have been reflecting upon. This should be simple faith sharing, with no discussion, and certainly no pressure on anyone to say anything.

Next, there is a short period of *shared prayer*. At this time we pray together—in thanksgiving, for help, for forgiveness, in support of one who has not experienced the loving activity of God—always in reference to what was shared in step three.

Finally, in step five, we say a *common prayer* together (the Our Father, for example, or a song) in order to bring our prayer to a close with a communal expression of praise and thanks to God.

When we get involved in communal reflection, it should be remembered and understood that we are not coming together to "render an account to one another." Nor are we giving progress reports. We come together in prayer: (a) *to remember* that we do, indeed, live in God's presence; (b) *to reflect* on our own consciousness—during a day or a week, with all of its varied activities—of the Divine Presence and to reflect on the influence that his presence has had on our way of acting; (c) *to share,* if we are so moved, the good news with our community: God at work in my life, redeeming me, making himself known to me and to those around me; (d) *to seek the support* and help of my community if I have found it difficult to be aware of the presence of God during the day, or if I have been unable to recognize it in myself, in others, or in the gifts of creation; (e) to reflect together on how we *as a group* have been able to witness to the saving presence of God in the world.

The more we are able to reflect personally and communally,

the more will we grow in our ability to *be present* to ourselves and to those around us, and the more will we be able to really open ourselves to growth in our awareness of God's presence everywhere.

QUESTIONS FOR COMMUNAL REFLECTION

The following are examples of the kind of question that could be used for communal reflection. Generally, the community would focus on only one question and spend twenty-five to forty minutes in this kind of prayer and faith sharing.

1. Have I been aware of the presence of God in my life? How has this presence been felt (experienced)?
2. How do I experience God's presence in the people around me?
3. What has been a recent experience of God's presence and activity in the world?
4. How have my interactions with others reflected the Lord's presence?
5. How do I find (experience) the Lord in the work I do?
6. Who is Christ for me in my day to day living?
7. How does the Lord make himself known to me through the Church?
8. How do I experience the Lord in this community?
9. How do I reflect the Lord to my family? my community? my co-workers? my Church?
10. Where have I experienced a block in my relationship to Christ recently?

8

THE CHRISTIAN
LIFE COMMUNITY MOVEMENT

*Come to him, to that living stone, rejected by men
but in God's sight chosen and precious; and like living stones be yourselves built into a spiritual house,
to be a holy priesthood, to offer spiritual sacrifices
acceptable to God through Jesus Christ.... You are
a chosen race, a royal priesthood, a holy nation,
God's own people, that you may declare the wonderful deeds of him who called you out of darkness into
his marvelous light. Once you were no people but
now you are God's people: once you had not received
mercy but now you have received mercy.*

1 Pet. 2:4–5, 9–10

The Faith Experience formats have been developed as a "community-building tool" by and for the Christian Life Community
movement. They are offered to the Church—to all people— by CLC
in hopes that this kind of faith sharing will help bring the human
family to a greater unity and to a greater sense of responsibility for
the life of all peoples on this planet. This chapter is written to tell
you something about the movement and about the spirituality and
vision of its members. We shall do this by looking at significant
turning points in its history, at its present development and the
struggles that come with that growth, and at some possibilities for
its future.

TURNING POINTS IN HISTORY

1540

The Christian Life Community movement has its roots, its origins, among the people who founded the Society of Jesus. In 1540,

St. Ignatius of Loyola had brought together a group of men who wanted to live a life of loving service in the Church. And from the very beginning, the Jesuits formed groups of adult men to help them in their ministry. These groups were called sodalities, the first of which was started by Blessed Peter Faber, the eldest of the sons of Ignatius, and was called the Sodality of the Holy Name of Jesus.

1563

In 1563, John Leunis, a Jesuit, began the Sodality of the Roman College and placed it under the protection of Our Lady of the Annunciation. This small group of students became what Pope Gregory XIII, in 1594, called "mother and head of all other sodalities on the face of the earth." It is impossible here to give more than a very brief sketch of the history of this movement, but that history is truly an amazing one.

At first, from 1540 to 1773, sodalities were formed wherever there was a Jesuit. Following the initial inspiration of Peter Faber and John Leunis, they were sources of spiritual life—occasions for growth in spirituality—and their members were intensely dedicated to apostolic service. Their goal was an integrated Christian life lived in an extraordinary way out of love for God and his people. And the sodalities did an immense amount of good: teaching catechism, working in prisons, ministering to the poor, caring for slaves, burying the dead, giving legal assistance, serving in hospitals, bringing peace to enemies, liberating prisoners, giving retreats, and printing and circulating pamphlets to help people understand their faith. All over the world sodalists gave outstanding example and support to those who wished to live Christianity in its fullness.

In his *Abridged History of the Sodalities of Our Lady* (The Queen's Work, St. Louis, 1956), Fr. Emile Villaret, S.J. writes that, once the sodality was definitely constituted and given papal approval and blessing,

> It never ceased to extend and increase its activity. It was found in all lands of ancient Christendom, and in the lands of the missions, in circles the most distinguished and the most lowly, practicing all the works of religion, of zeal, and of charity, ceaselessly attentive so as to be ready to respond to current needs. The most encouraging encomiums,

the most violent attacks bear witness to its importance and
its success (p. 96).

It is estimated that by 1773 there were 2,500 groups in this world-
wide movement.

1773

The year 1773 marked a turning point for the movement because it was in that year that the Society of Jesus was suppressed.
The sodalities had been under the exclusive authority of the General of the Society, and only Jesuits could be "directors" of those
groups. But so important to the Church had sodalities become that
the Pope who suppressed the Society of Jesus also went to great
pains to continue the existence of the sodalities without them.

Fr. Louis Paulussen, S.J., who in 1950 became the director of
the World Sodality Secretariat in Rome and subsequently the
founder of the World Federation (first of Sodalities, and then of the
Christian Life Community movement as we know it today), ob-
served in the January 1974 issue of the WFCLC publication
Progressio that the suppression of the Jesuits had a tremendously
negative impact on the future of the sodalities:

> It would have been a miracle if many groups had not lost
> their identity. The change of spiritual guides was too dras-
> tic, too sudden. No wonder that this period is in many ways
> the opposite of the first one. This was especially true in the
> late nineteenth and the twentieth century. In these years
> many bishops wanted the sodalities as their parish associ-
> ation, too often only to foster a rather individualistic piety.
> Still more unfortunate was the fact that numerous youth
> associations "organized" sodalities or even imposed it from
> above, frequently having as their principal aim protecting
> their members from evil. The fast growth of these years
> was unnatural, and a deadly danger for the authentic spir-
> it. More than 80,000 groups were affiliated in these years,
> very often without reference to Ignatian spirituality. After
> the restoration of the Society (1814), the Jesuits were again
> charged with sodalities, but the true spirit did not always
> return with them. No need to say it, here and there excel-
> lent groups did wonderful work. And also the many groups
> existing almost everywhere did some good. But as a whole,
> the movement had lost the original spirit.

1948

Pope Pius XII, who called himself the Pope-Sodalist, gave extraordinary help to this movement in 1948 by issuing an Apostolic Constitution (*Bis Saeculari*) in which he affirmed the sodalities as an "outstanding and particular form of Catholic Action." This document was a catalyst to the growth that has seen the sodality mature into its present form. In its challenge to renewal, to a return to the original, outstanding inspiration of its early years, it insisted on the urgent need for an international community of people who would be able to reflect upon and deal with international situations in order to bring the message and values of Christ to all people.

Fr. Paulussen (*op. cit.*) writes:

> After the publication of *Bis Saeculari* all those endless discussions on our identity became silent. The new image of the sodalities was clear, much clearer than in any other document of the past. As in the Exercises the whole spirituality is centered on Christ. As in the rules of the first group in 1574, the aim is the Christian life in its fullness and in all its dimensions. All are invited "to grow gently to a high level in the life of the Spirit, even to sanctity...." All means are concentrated on the "perfect and wholehearted following of Christ."

1967

Between the years 1948 and 1967 came the formation of the World Federation, and a concerted effort at discovering and implementing the implications of Pius XII's prophetic challenge to become a world community. These were also years of great change in the world and in the Church. The inspiration of the Second Vatican Council took root quickly in the hearts of these sodalists who were trying to respond to the call of Christ in their day. And so, it was not until 1967, two years after the close of the Council, that the World Federation of Sodalities was able to formulate what can be called the contemporary expression of the original vision of Ignatius and Faber and Leunis.

In 1967, at the World Sodality Congress in Rome, the new "General Principles" were approved and a new name—Christian Life Communities—was adopted. A rebirth took place—a world community, given new life by the Church it has always sought to serve and by a return to its sources and its original spirituality. Indeed, the growth that has taken place since that significant World Congress has been the fruit of a long, often very difficult, struggle to truly be a world community at the service of one world.

The basic elements of the new General Principles, which were given final ecclesial approval by Pope Paul VI in 1971, are the following:

> Christian Life Communities aim to develop and sustain men and women, adults and youth, who commit themselves to the service of the Church and the world in every area of life. . . .

> Our Communities are for all who feel the urgent need to unite their human life in all its dimensions with the fullness of their Christian faith. . . .

> Our spirituality is ecclesial—centered on Christ and on participation in the paschal mystery. . . .

> The Spiritual Exercises of St. Ignatius are a specific source and the characteristic instrument of our spirituality. . . .

> We seek to work for the reform of structures of society, to participate actively in vital efforts to eliminate the causes of injustice, to win liberation for victims of discrimination of any kind, and to strive to overcome the widening differences between rich and poor within the Church and wherever they exist. . . .

> Mary holds a special place in CLC as the model of total openness to God's Spirit which is visible in her continual cooperation in the work of Jesus, the Christ, Liberator of mankind. . . .

GROWTH AND DEVELOPMENT

I think the struggle of the Christian Life Community movement has something to do with each of the preceding chapters of this book. Part of our present-day struggle involves our history and our need to be "in touch" with the great heritage that is ours. Our history tells us that our members are outstanding in their commitment to Christ and to the service of his people; that the source of our inspiration includes the spirituality of our founders, a spirituality flowing out of the Spiritual Exercises of St. Ignatius; that to be of real service, we have to be rooted in our own day, willing and eager to move with the times, to adapt and renew with our Church, even at times to be prophetic voices in the world; that among our primary ends are included every form of apostolate, particularly the social apostolate; that our groups are devoted to and stand under the protection of Mary, the mother of God and the mother of all people.

The struggle of today's CLC movement is one that has to do with being a vibrant part of the Church, willing to participate in the paschal mystery of Jesus. With groups in over fifty countries, this world community is part of the suffering Church, part of the silenced church, part of the persecuted Church, part of the missionary Church. Our members are mostly adult lay Christians who seek to take an adult Christian stance in today's world. This means that we are striving more and more to become discerning communities for service, listening to the many calls of the Lord, espousing the values proclaimed by Jesus in the Beatitudes, attentive to the struggle for justice everywhere in the world. And we are becoming more and more willing to let our lifestyles be affected by our beliefs and by our deepest desires for the liberation of the world.

One way to see how CLC is growing is to look at the way the vision of the movement is articulated and refined by the World Assemblies (held every three years) and by the U.S. National Federation, especially through its biennial conventions.

1973

It was in Augsburg, Germany, in 1973, that the World CLC Movement took a significant step in a new direction. CLC representatives from some forty countries came together to look at, discuss, reflect upon, and pray about the place of CLC in the Church and in the world. The work that was done in Augsburg could never have been done by a single group or by an individual national federation. What was needed was a sharing of the talents, insights, experiences, struggles and richness of a world community. What emerged was a common vision of CLC as "a community at the service of the liberation of the whole person and of all people."

That same year, 1973, was the year of a significant step taken in the United States. Less than a week after the World Assembly in Augsburg, over four hundred people assembled in Iowa City for the National Convention. The theme for this gathering was "New Communities for Christians—An American Response." Participants were challenged to look at the American Church and at CLC's place in that Church, and a commitment was made to foster the growth of Christian community in the United States. Since that time, a number of individuals and groups have been actively involved in local and diocesan efforts to promote communities of Christians committed to the service of God's people.

1975

The theme of the 1975 National Convention, held in Amherst, Massachusetts, was "Reconciliation and Liberation Through Christian Community." This was an attempt to further deepen the work begun in 1973. Universal liberation (Augsburg) and reconciliation (theme for the Church's Holy Year) are possible, we believe, through Christian community (Iowa City). American CLC's have grown in their conviction that they have a unique contribution to make to the Church. One example is the development of a formation program which provides tools needed to develop the kind of community (whether CLC or not) that will truly reconcile us to one another and free us to live with the dignity of God's children.

1976

In the summer of 1976, in Manila, the Philippines, the World Community gathered once again—this time to consider the theme, "Poor with Christ for a Better Service—The Vocation of CLC in the Mission of the Church." The growth taking place is evident in the statement of orientation or direction that the delegates committed themselves to as a result of that assembly:

> The CLC's are aware that they have rediscovered their specific nature in the path of the Spiritual Exercises; this they now confirm. They confirm too the orientation taken at Augsburg in favor of a commitment to the liberation of the whole person and of all people. But the continuation of this direction is now matched by the very widespread option of a preference for the poor, an option that must express itself in a concrete insertion and a service with and for the poor.

1977

The year 1977 was a major turning point for the Christian Life Communities in the United States. Two major events highlight what had been happening to the people who were living out of this vision and spirituality. The first was the National Convention. Held in New Orleans, it developed the theme, "Gifted in the Lord—Ministers in His Kingdom." More than five hundred people gathered to consider the world and its needs, as well as to respond to the challenge to use our God-given gifts in ministry to his people. A real conversion seems to have taken place at that meeting. A renewed movement was beginning to understand its heritage and its mission, as an entire national community was beginning to turn its gaze outward to the world in which we are called to be servants.

Two months after the convention, the leadership of CLC in the United States spent three days in an intense discernment process to see how it might be possible to live out the vision of the World Movement within the context of the North American experience. What came out of that meeting was a clarity of vision and purpose that had not been articulated before. The leadership issued a statement that has since become an accepted statement of purpose, not just for the leaders, but for the movement in general in the United States:

> The Leadership Community of NFCLC has made its own the thrust given by the World Federation in its last general assembly in Manila, 1976, namely, "Poor with Christ for a Better Service." It is the purpose of this community, then, to make this vision come alive in this country by radicalizing in Christ—by an integrated Ignatian spirituality—the vision, values, lifestyles and commitment to action of its members and member communities, therefore coming to the fullest realization of our vocation within the American experience today.

1978

In July 1978 fifty leaders of the CLC movement in the United States met for five days to consider the mission of CLC in this country. This "national deliberation" focused on a number of elements involved in the ministry of justice and liberation in our world. The leaders came away from that deliberation convinced that if we are to be effective in living out the vision and purpose of this movement, we must simultaneously (a) *educate* ourselves *for justice* so that we may understand the issues, (b) submit our *lifestyles* to a close scrutiny so that we may truly be living the Gospel values we proclaim, (c) be involved in *direct action for justice* so that we may not simply become study groups, (d) reflect on our activity in light of our *spirituality* so that we may more faithfully integrate these two dimensions of our lives, (e) participate in true *evangelization* so that we may share with others the lived beliefs of our movement, and (f) *network* our efforts so that we may more effectively communicate among ourselves and cooperate with other people of good will in promoting justice in the world.

1979

A second deliberation was held within six months of the first. In February 1979 seventy-five CLC members gathered in St. Louis to develop ways of communicating the fruit of Deliberation I to those who would participate in the 1979 National CLC Convention. Once again, the creativity and vision of those people resulted in a clearer understanding of the CLC movement and a stronger commitment to its ideals and goals.

The theme for convention '79, held in San Francisco, was "The cry of the people has come to me." Inspired by God's compassion and promise of liberation (Ex. 3:7–10) and moved by the tremendous sufferings of people all over the world, the CLC movement recommitted itself to a careful, caring listening to God's people and to a unified, active proclamation of, and participation in, God's liberation of all peoples.

THE FUTURE

What is the future of Christian Life Communities? If we remain true to our vision, we will continue a deepening process that will change us as individuals and bring back to us, as a community, the zeal and enthusiasm for service that animated our earliest members.

The World Federation of Christian Life Communities is expending its energy toward the development of "A World Community at the Service of One World." This was the theme for the 1979 World Assembly in Rome. It is a brave response to the call of the Church to care for our world and to foster a consciousness of that world as the dwelling place of the human family and of our God. The vision of Fr. Paulussen at the foundation of the World Federation in 1953 is becoming more and more of a reality. In reflecting in the January 1974 issue of *Progressio* on how the renewal of the movement had "pushed (us) irresistibly to the great question of the Exercises," Fr. Paulussen wrote:

> The question "What does God want *us* to do?" does not make sense unless *we* are able to do something. This implies that we are united—and not only spiritually—in a permanent way. This means World Federation: a concrete possibility for deliberation and action on the world level.

In part, our future as a movement lies in our ability and our willingness to look at international issues and to act as one world community motivated by the Christian ideal of the liberation of all people.

The same is true in the United States. The future calls us to develop the National Federation in such a way that we will be able to speak and to act as one body, and to bring the richness and resourcefulness of our membership to the efforts of the Church and of all people of good will in making this a just society.

At both the international and the national levels, we have developed formation materials which can help people grow in spirituality and in their awareness of the needs of the human family. We have a large number of CLC members, lay and religious, whose apostolic work includes guiding people through the Spiritual Exercises and giving spiritual direction. We have NGO (Non-Governmental Organization) status at the United Nations, as well as delegates who are exercising a good deal of influence in that international body. In the United States we have ties with a number of groups or organizations whose main interest is education for justice or direct action for justice. One of our concerns is the integration of spirituality and justice, and we try to bring that integration to the work we are doing.

Most importantly, we have people. The dynamic movement of the past, begun more than four hundred years ago, found its greatest inspiration and hope for the future in the people who were committed to this radical way of living. Fr. Villaret's history of the movement points to a membership down through the years that includes "at least thirty-two canonized saints ... thirty-seven founders or foundresses of religious orders or congregations ... two

Doctors of the Universal Church (Francis de Sales and Alphonsus Liguori) . . . martyrs from every land . . . eighteen Popes . . . kings, emperors, prince-regents of Austria, Bavaria, Spain, France, Portugal, Saxony, Savòy. . . . In every department of the intellectual life, in letters, science, the arts, we see brilliant lights (including the physicist, Volta; the composer, Mozart; and two great painters, Van Dyck and Rubens)."

Villaret continues:

> Above all intellectual, social, military, and political activity, we must render homage to that which is charitable and apostolic. Now this is so identified with the very life of the sodality that it unfolds in a deeper obscurity; it prints in large type fewer dazzling names known all over the world. On the other hand, those whom we could justly cite and whose renown does not go beyond the limits of their own city or province would furnish us with a list that could go on forever. . . . More hidden still from the great world are the sodalists who have devoted themselves to the poor, the sick, the cancerous, the lepers. . . . But especially ignored by nearly everybody are they who were splendid in the practice of their duties and their daily apostolate. Circumstances have thrown a light around the great figure of the workingman, Matt Talbot; they could have thrown an equal light on legions of others.

Now in our day, our greatest hope is also in our people—in families, in schools, in religious communities, in law and politics, in medicine and the social sciences, in education, the arts, and business, in all walks of life, at every level of society. (Of the challenges given by the World Federation, perhaps the most significant for us is the establishment of groups among the poor. We have come to realize that the movement must be able to learn from the poor and to be available to the poor.) Our members are people whose lives are animated by the spirit of Jesus and nourished by their participation in the Church and by the Spiritual Exercises of St. Ignatius, and who have banded together in small Christian communities for mutual support and challenge in living a true Christian life.

We have a history and a rich heritage that is part, even now, of the "Contemporary Testament." We are part of the Church and we live, in our day-to-day lives, the paschal mystery of Jesus Christ. We believe that we are called by name by our God, and that our call has something to do with becoming a Beatitude people, a people committed to living radical Christianity and to working for the liberation of the whole person and of all people.

We will share our faith with all who care to listen and to share with us, because we believe that the news is good and worthy of being celebrated in this life—in this world.